Hemingway's Cats

Hemingway relaxes with best cat friend, Boise, on the terrace of his Cuban home.

Hemingway's Cats

Carlene Fredericka Brennen

Foreword by Hilary Hemingway

Pineapple Press, Inc.
Sarasota, Florida

Also by Carlene Fredericka Brennen

Books

Hemingway in Cuba
with Hilary Hemingway

*Randy Wayne White's Gulf Coast Cookbook with
Memories and Photos of Sanibel Island*
with Randy Wayne White

*Tarpon Tales:
Lost Stories and Research 1899–1939*
with Randy Wayne White

*Randy Wayne White's
Ultimate Tarpon Book:
The Birth of Big Game Fishing*
with Randy Wayne White

Documentaries

*Hemingway in Cuba
The Birth of Big Game Fishing
Hemingway's Cats*

Inquiries should be addressed to:

Pineapple Press, Inc.
P.O. Box 3889
Sarasota, Florida 34230

www.pineapplepress.com

Library of Congress Cataloging-in-Publication Data

Brennen, Carlene.
  Hemingway's cats / by Carlene Fredericka Brennen ; foreword by Hilary Hemingway.—
    p. cm.
  Includes bibliographical references (p.   ) and index.
  ISBN-13: 978-1-56164-342-4 (hardback : alk. paper)
  ISBN-13: 978-1-56164-489-6 (paperback : alk. paper)
  1. Hemingway, Ernest, 1899-1961. 2. Authors, American—20th century—Biography. 3. Human-animal relationships—United States. 4. Journalists—United States—Biography. 5. Cat owners—United States—Biography. 6. Cats—United States—Anecdotes. I. Title.
  PS3515.E37Z58256 2005
  813'.52—dc22

                                2005017185

10 9 8 7 6 5 4 3 2 1

Printed in the United States of America

Hemingway at home in Cuba with his sons, Patrick and Gregory, and their kittens, Good Will, Princessa, and Boise

Cristóbal's place during meals was on the table to the right of Hemingway's chair.

To my beloved daughter
Shamlene (Shamie) Kelly,
who was the heart and soul
behind this book

In Memory

—Of my parents Glenda and Bill Semmer, whose love and
encouragement knew no bounds. Because of their deep devotion to their
family pets, they would have considered this project worthwhile.

—Of my cat Norman, my dearest cat friend, a black and white Sanibel Island cat
who gave me ten years of unquestionable loyalty, devotion, and love. Norman
walked with me as a dog walks, slept on my pillow or by my side, sat on my desk
as I wrote or in my lap as I read, giving me, as Hemingway would say, "valuable aid."

. . . men of kindly impulse take up with pets for they must love something.
— Mark Twain

Table of Contents

Foreword by Hilary Hemingway xi

Author's Note xiii

1. The Early Cat Years 1

2. Cats at Walloon Lake 5

3. Love and War 9

4. The First Mrs. Hemingway 13

5. Too Poor to Own a Cat 15

6. Paris and Feather Puss 19

7. A Feather Kitty Never Dies 23

8. The Isle of Cats 27

9. Key West—The Cats Next Door 33

10. Not a Cat Fancier 39

11. The Stray Cats of Finca Vigia 45

12. Hemingway's Dearest Cat Friends 47

13. Negrita Finds a Home 57

14. The Circus Cats 65

15. No Cats on the *Pilar* 69

Hemingway enjoying breakfast with his cats in Cuba.

16. A Wildcat in Bed   79

17. Mary Welsh and the Cats' Tower   81

18. Miss Kitty of the Wild West   91

19. Never Punish a Cat   95

20. Finding Black Dog   99

21. The Cat Wars   107

22. Pets, Guns, and the Pulitzer Prize   111

23. African Wildlife and Two Airplane Crashes   117

24. Cats, Dogs, and the Nobel Prize   125

25. Boise Remembered   127

26. The Next Household Cat Prince   133

27. The Loss of Black Dog   135

28. Two Cats and an Owl   139

29. "Your Big Kitten" in Cuba and Spain   147

30. Without His Cats   151

31. "Good Night, My Kitten"   155

32. Fidel Castro and the Last of the Finca Cats   159

Hemingway and Black Dog in the Finca living room.

Mary and Ernest Hemingway with Black Dog in Cuba.

The Cast of Cats   164

The Cast of Dogs   172

Other Animals   174

Acknowledgments   175

Bibliography   179

Photo Credits   186

Permissions   187

Index   191

Hemingway working at the Finca with Black Dog by his side.

Foreword

by Hilary Hemingway

The image most people have of Ernest Hemingway is that of a macho hunter and fisherman. In fact, most historical photographs of the great author seem to reinforce this misconception. When Carlene Fredericka Brennen asked that I write a foreword on his devotion to his many cats and dogs, I was pleased to see that she also included her valuable scholarship on Hemingway's understanding of nature. There is no question that when Papa was hiking along winding rivers to take a fish on fly, or watching his prey in the African bush, he was always working to better his understanding of animals. He studied their natural habitat, analyzed their migration and feeding habits, watched the physical changes over their lifespan and, like John Audubon, Hemingway often killed the animals he studied. He examined them in life, and in death, and his writing always included that mystical bond between the hunter and the hunted. As Santiago expressed in *The Old Man and the Sea,* he had great love and admiration for the fish, even as he was determined to kill it.

Hilary Hemingway at Ernest's Key West home

But what of the animals Hemingway chose to keep at his homes? When you hear of Hemingway and Key West, you immediately imagine a yardful of six-toed cats. Why? Brennen answers this with her beautifully illustrated work that shows Papa's love for the domestic feline, as well as his canine friends.

Key West was not the only town known for Hemingway cats. In Cuba, Ernest's hilltop home, Finca Vigia (Lookout Farm), once had fifty-seven cats and twelve dogs roaming its grounds. One of the first cats Hemingway purchased in Cuba was a Persian female named Tester that came from the Silver Dawn Cattery in Florida. Tester was renamed Princessa by the Finca staff because of her elegant nature. Later Princessa mated with Boise—whom Papa first called Dillinger—a Cuban kitten he had found and adopted from the coastal fishing village of Cojimar. By the end of the first summer, he owned three house cats: Princessa, Boise, and a half-Maltese kitten named Willy.

Ernest took great pleasure in writing to his family about his cats and how they were getting along. By 1943, Ernest and third wife Martha had eleven cats at Finca Vigia. *"One cat just leads to another . . ."* Hemingway wrote to his first wife, Hadley Mowrer. *"The place is so damned big it doesn't really seem as though there were many cats until you see them all moving like a mass migration at feeding time. . . . It is wonderful when Marty, and /or kids are here but is lonesome as a bastard when I'm here alone. I have taught Uncle Wolfer, Dillinger and Will to walk along the railings to the top of the porch pillars and make a pyramid like lions and have taught Friendless to drink with me (whiskey and milk) but even that doesn't take the place of a wife and family."*

Ernest later uses his isolation from his family and his kinship with his cats as inspiration for his hero, Thomas Hudson, in his novel, *Islands in the Stream*. Hudson talks to his cats and was comforted by them after learning of his sons' tragic deaths in a car accident. Princessa is elegant and aristocratic, while Boise is the male cat who hunts fruit rats and is devoted to Thomas Hudson. Goats (aka Bigotes, Friendless) is the fighter and stud cat. All three cats are immortalized in this novel.

By the time Papa's fourth wife-to-be, Mary Welsh, moved into the Finca in 1945, Ernest had twenty-three cats and five dogs. They were treated as royalty. The cats slept in the guest bedroom and later lived in a room on the second floor of the white tower Papa had built for his cats at one end of the terrace. He and Mary called the cats "purr factories" and "love sponges" that soaked up their love and in return gave them comfort and companionship. Hemingway's beloved Black Dog, an adopted stray from Ketchum Idaho, slept beside his bed; Negrita, a stray from the streets of Havana slept on Mary's side of the bed; and his best friend Boise rested comfortably on his chest.

Among the many family letters describing his cats and dogs is one written in 1942. Ernest tells Hadley Mowrer that he had not been able to sleep the night before and had recalled a song they had composed for their cat, F. Puss, so many years earlier in Paris. It went like this, *"A feather kitty's talent lies / In scratching out the other's eyes. A feather kitty never dies / Oh immortality."* According to the letter, the Finca cats enjoyed Papa's song.

On behalf of my family, I hope you enjoy Carlene Fredericka Brennen's illustrated text on *Hemingway's Cats*.

—Hilary Hemingway

The author with Norman

Author's Note

As a cat aficionado and the owner of three cats, I was intrigued by Ernest Hemingway's deep devotion to the family pets. The more I researched this complex writer's life and his close association with animals, the more I came to understand Hemingway the man, the lover, the husband, the father, the hunter, the fisherman, the writer, as well as the devoted master of many cats and dogs. I discovered a kinder, gentler, man known only to a family and close friends, quite different from the macho character he himself helped to create – a man part fact, part fiction.

Hemingway adopted stray cats in every city where he lived, owning fifty-seven cats in Cuba and two in Idaho when he died. It had been his animals that often kept him company while he wrote and helped him to cope with his failing relationships, deep-seated loneliness and life threatening illnesses, and when he took his life on July 2nd, 1961, his cat Big Boy Peterson was by his side.

Carlene Fredericka Brennen
www.hemingwayscats.com

The Hemingway family, left to right: Marcelline, Sunny, Dr. Clarence and Grace Hemingway, Ursula, and Ernest

chapter 1

The Early Cat Years

I have felt profound affection for three
different cats, four dogs, that I remember,
and only two horses; that is horses that I
owned, ridden or driven.

Death in the Afternoon

"Cats are the natural companions of intellectuals. They are silent watchers of dreams, inspiration and patient research," wrote French veterinarian Dr. Fernand Mery in his 1966 book *The Life, History and Magic of the Cat.* Nobel Prize–winning author Ernest Hemingway could very well be Dr. Mery's prime example.

Ernest Hemingway inherited his love for animals from his parents—Grace Hall, a devoted cat fancier, and Clarence Edmonds (Ed) Hemingway, once an aspiring veterinarian before he focused on a single species, *Homo sapiens,* to serve as a medical practitioner and surgeon. However, it wasn't unusual for Dr. Hemingway, despite his busy schedule, to offer his services to neighbors when their pets were in need of medical assistance.

Ernest's sister, Marcelline Hemingway Sanford, recalled in her book, *At the Hemingways,* that she'd always heard that her father, even as a small boy, would put splints on a wounded creature's leg or wing and feed orphaned animals, hoping to keep them healthy until they reached an independent life. So it wasn't surprising that Dr. Hemingway once rushed to the rescue of one of Ernest's favorite cats.

". . . an outside door . . . slammed during a windstorm and cut our poor cat's tail right off. There was the cat squealing under a chair on the porch and inside was most of his tail," recalled Ernest's sister, Madelaine Hemingway Miller, in her book *Ernie Hemingway's Sister "Sunny" Remembers.* "Thankfully he healed well after Daddy's expert emergency treatment. Whatever the cat had been christened escapes me, but from that time on he was known as Manx."

Above: Ernest feeding a squirrel, 1910
Below: Hemingway's birthplace home at
439 N. Oak Park Avenue in Oak Park,
Illinois

Dr. Hemingway passed on to Ernest not only his skills of animal doctoring, but his knowledge and love of nature. "Ernest was fond of all animals including wild ones," his mother Grace once said. "He is a natural scientist, loving everything in the ways of bugs, shells, birds, animals, insects, and blossoms." By the age of three, Ernest surprised his parents by correctly identifying seventy-three birds in his father's *Birds of Nature* volume.

Ernest's grandfather, Ernest (Abba) Hall, whom Ernest loved and was proud to have been named after, also had a fondness for animals. After Hall's wife, Caroline Hancock, died of cancer, Hall found comfort with his beloved white Yorkshire terrier, Tassel, whom Ernest adored. This was a family trait Ernest would inherit. He often sought comfort and love from his cats and dogs during some of the loneliest and most stressful times of his life.

Above: Ernest, Grandfather Ernest (Abba) Hall, Marcelline, and Ursula
Below: Dr. Clarence Hemingway's horse and buggy; one of Ernest's responsibilities was to help care for the horse.

Grandfather Hall's kindness to animals was legendary and left a lasting impression on Ernest. According to Ernest's sister, Marcelline, Hall once witnessed a junkman beating his old horse. After some lengthy negotiations, Hall purchased the horse and put it out to pasture, where it grazed and lived until its death. Ernest would also be known for rescuing mistreated and unwanted animals and adopting stray cats and dogs throughout his life. According to Dr. Marty Becker in his book *The Healing Power of Pets:* "Children's interest in pets is the one strong element of childhood that survives as they mature. . . ."

Hemingway would write in his book *Death in the Afternoon,* published in 1932, how when seeing horses in distress he was compelled to assist the noble animals:

> *I cannot see a horse down in the street without having it make me feel a necessity for helping the horse, and I have spread sacking, unbuckled harness and dodged shod hoofs many times and will again if they have horses on city streets in wet and ice weather. . . .*

Ernest, as did his father and grandfather before him, would pass on to his children his unselfish devotion to the family pets.

Hemingway had a natural understanding of animals. His low voice and quiet manner appealed to his animal friends, creating bonds that lasted throughout his life. Ernest would later write about these friendships in his books *Death in the Afternoon,*

Islands in the Stream, A Moveable Feast, The Garden of Eden, and *True at First Light.*

"People remember their relationship with their first pet as taking place in a simple time in their lives, even though most of what you go through growing up is far from simple," wrote Dr. Marty Becker. "As kids, we try to find a pattern in all of the stimuli; decide what to trust and what to fear, and along the way experience our first joy, connection, rejection, loneliness and heartbreak. We face some of our largest and most memorable triumphs. Frequently, the companionship of pets is the constant that gets us through." Hemingway would rely on his pets throughout his life to help him through some of his most difficult times.

Left to right (top row): Ernest, Dr. Clarence and Grace Hemingway; (bottom row): Ursula, Sunny, and Marcelline

Grace Hemingway shows her catch to Ernest, Ursula, and Marcelline while at their cottage at Walloon Lake.

chapter 2

Cats at Walloon Lake

*. . . some nights I would try to remember all the animals
in the world by name and then the birds and then the
fishes . . . and when I could not remember anything at all
anymore I would just listen.*

Now I Lay Me

During Ernest's childhood and teenage years, the Hemingway family would pack up and move from their home in Oak Park, Illinois, leaving behind their ever-growing menagerie in the care of a servant, and spend three months at their summer cottage, Windermere, on Walloon Lake in Upper Michigan. Before leaving the city, Ernest and his sisters would check out enough books from the Oak Park Library to last them throughout the summer months. Ernest's sister, Madelaine, remembered that Ernest took the most books to read, including books by Stephen Crane, Robert Louis Stevenson, Rudyard Kipling, and his favorite author, Mark Twain, whose love of animals, especially cats, was legendary.

"Ernest loved adventure fiction and next to that, science. . . . he read constantly even though his eyesight was poor," Leicester Hemingway wrote in his biography *My Brother, Ernest Hemingway.*

The summer getaway was a wonderful time of beach picnics, boat rides, swimming, fishing, hunting, marshmallow roasts, barn raisings, and long hours of relaxation and reading. The only thing missing was the companionship of their beloved cats at home in Oak Park.

Ernest's sister, Carol Hemingway Gardner, recalled a humorous incident with their mother, Grace, and the family's

*Above: The Hemingway's new house at 600 N. Kenilworth Avenue, Oak Park, Illinois, 1906
Below: Cats were considered members of the family.*

cats. The Hemingways were traveling by train to their cottage in Upper Michigan. Grace had decided that one of their cats, Catherine Tiger, and her young kittens, would also make the trip, possibly at the requests of Ernest and his siblings. The cat family was hidden in a carry-all amongst the luggage.

Kittens were always around to entertain.

The family cats also made the trips to the summer cottage.

The conductor, upon hearing the hungry cry of one of the kittens, questioned the family, asking whether they had an animal on board. Carol's mother, Grace, stood up, straight and tall, her large frame concealing the basket of kittens and, in her most imposing manner, asked the conductor if he thought she would bring an animal into a sleeping car. The conductor immediately retreated. Catherine Tiger and her kittens were then safely hidden away in Carol's upper berth for the rest of the trip. Carol believed the porter knew about the cat family, but she suspected her father had probably tipped him generously. Young Ernest may have named the independent feline after Catherine the Great, a historic figure he had read about and greatly admired. It was a name he would later use again and again when writing about strong female characters in his novels.

According to Dr. Marty Becker in his book *The Healing Power of Pets:* "Those who bond with animals from the ages of birth to five and later between the early adolescent ages of twelve to fifteen experience a long-term benefit from the relationship. . . . people who had pets with whom they were especially close during those times of change later had a generally more positive sense of themselves, particularly adolescents."

Ernest's sister Madelaine said that she and Ernest always managed to collect a variety of pets while at the lake, including kittens from neighboring farms. Not only did these loveable creatures become attentive playmates but, as they grew older, the cats helped to keep down the menacing mouse population at the cottage, a battle Dr. Hemingway seemed to be losing.

If a cat or kitten succumbed from illness or accident, a lovely burial was performed. A shoebox would be used as a coffin and placed in an area of the yard designated as the pet graveyard. The girls would solemnly march around the gravesite, playing music from hand-wound music boxes. Dead songbirds were also given the same preferential treatment. Madelaine remembered that Ernest would attend the ceremonies but did not participate.

Ernest became a skilled fisherman under the tutelage of his father, Clarence, spending many happy days fishing the nearby creeks, rivers, and lakes. In his short story, "Now I Lay Me," he recalled a day when as a boy he ran out of bait and the sensitivity he felt toward a creature he put on his hook in hopes of catching a trout.

Often I ran out of bait because I would take only ten worms with me in a tobacco tin when I started. . . . Sometimes I found insects in the swamp meadows. . . . There were beetles and insects with legs like grass stems, and grubs in old rotten logs. . . . Once I used a salamander from under an old log. The salamander was very small and neat and agile and a lovely color. He had tiny feet and tried to hold on to the hook, and after that one time I never used a salamander, although I found them very often. Nor did I use crickets, because of the way they acted about the hook.

At night Ernest preferred sleeping in a tent outside the crowded cottage and would often read, by kerosene lamp, late into the night. The cats and kittens of Windermere became his cherished companions. Ernest would often rely on memories from his childhood past when expressing a certain feeling or situation in his short stories and novels. The summers at Walloon Lake were some of the happiest times of Ernest's life, and he would recall these memories in his work over and over again, as he may have done in this passage from *Islands in the Stream:*

The floor hardened against his right hip and his thigh and right shoulder, so he lay on his back now and rested against the muscles of his shoulders, drawing his knees up under the blankets and letting his heels push against the blanket. This took some of the tiredness out of his body and he put his left hand on the sleeping cat and stroked him.

Ernest would return to the cottage at Windermere as a young adult, but his days there as a child would leave a lasting memory.

Ernest and his mother Grace preparing for a trip, 1910

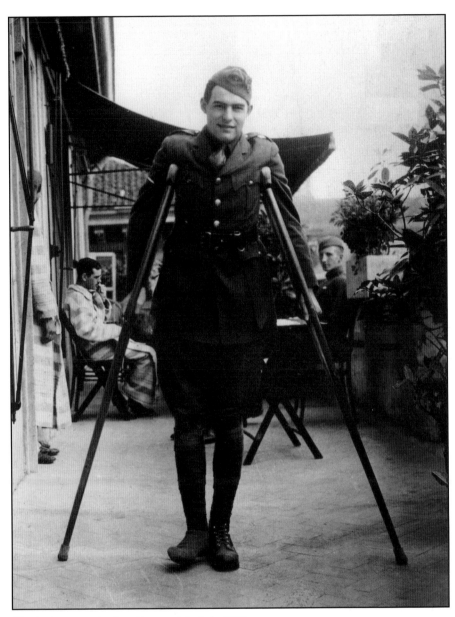

Hemingway recovering from his wounds in Italy, 1918

chapter 3

Love and War

Maybe cats do not die. . . . they say,
they have nine lives, I do not know,
but most men die like animals,
not like men.

A Natural History of the World

Ernest Hemingway graduated from Oak Park
and River Forest Township High School in June
1917. Writing for the high school weekly paper,
The Trapeze, and the school literary magazine,
Tabula, fueled his desire to become a writer.

After graduation Hemingway considered
enlisting in the army. The war was escalating in
Europe and he wanted to be part of it. Henry S.
Villard, who was a patient in the hospital with
Ernest in Italy, wrote in *Hemingway in Love and
War: The Lost Diary of Agnes von Kurowsky:* "To
many of us the war in Europe resembled a gigantic
stage on which the most exciting drama ever
produced was being played out." But, because of
his age, Ernest's parents refused to give him the
permission needed. They still had hopes that he
would attend Oberlin College, where his father had
graduated prior to earning his M.D. at Chicago's
Rush Medical College.

Ernest knew he wanted to be a writer, and he
could not see postponing his career to spend four
more years in school. Later in life he would say he
regretted never having gone to college.

Ernest's Uncle Alfred Tyler Hemingway offered
his help and, through his connections, he was able
to secure a job for his nephew as a cub reporter
with the *Kansas City Star.* Working with some
of the top reporters and editors at the paper,
Hemingway learned the skills of a journalist.

While on assignment for the newspaper,
Hemingway interviewed officers with the Red
Cross who were looking for volunteers to drive
ambulances in Italy. Hemingway immediately

*Above: Ernest in his soldier's uniform,
1918 Below: Red Cross nurse Agnes
von Kurowsky, Hemingway's first true
love, 1918*

9

signed up, ending his six-month apprenticeship with the *Star*.

Ernest departed from New York City on May 23, 1918, and arrived in Italy on June 4. The lazy summer days at Windermere on Walloon Lake—fishing, reading, and relaxing with the family cats at his side—must have seemed a distant memory.

Hemingway's job primarily consisted of driving ambulances and evacuating the wounded. When the Red Cross needed men to deliver candy, cigarettes, and mail to the soldiers on the front lines, Hemingway volunteered. But his time at the front proved short-lived. On July 8, just thirteen days short of his nineteenth birthday, a trench mortar exploded near Hemingway, killing one soldier and seriously injuring two others. Not realizing the extent of his own wounds, Hemingway, with over two hundred shrapnel wounds in his legs (he would later describe the pain as the sting of a thousand hornets), lifted one of the wounded soldiers onto his back and dragged the soldier a hundred and fifty yards through a barrage of machine gun bullets to a first aid post. Hemingway's uniform, soaked in the injured soldier's blood, gave evidence that the soldier's body may have shielded Hemingway from becoming fatally wounded. The Italian soldiers were amazed by the young American's bravery.

Hemingway would endure two surgeries to remove 237 pieces of shrapnel from his hands and legs, and bullets from behind his right and left knees and his right foot. There were so many wounds that his doctors considered amputation. A large scar on his right foot left Hemingway a permanent reminder of the war.

Promoted to first lieutenant, Hemingway became the first American to be wounded in Italy, receiving the Legion of Honor Medal and the Silver Medal of Valor, one of Italy's highest honors. Biographer James R. Mellow wrote in his book *Hemingway: A Life Without Consequences,* " . . . it would take years before Hemingway's brush with death, the traumatic experience of being wounded, would leave his mind."

During Hemingway's childhood, it had been his sisters and the family cats that kept him company when he was sick in bed. In the American Red Cross Hospital in Milan, Italy, it was visiting American and Italian soldiers, fellow Red Cross workers, and the hospital staff, who all helped to cheer up the young patient so far from home.

It was during this time that Hemingway met and fell in love with his nurse, Agnes Hannah von Kurowsky, fondly called Von by her friends. Agnes, an American from Washington, D.C., was a former librarian and a registered nurse. After graduating from nursing school she had joined the Red Cross Nursing Service and applied for a job in Europe.

During Hemingway's childhood, the cats and kittens had kept him company when he was sick in bed.

Like most wartime romances, their relationship quickly progressed. In Agnes's diary, she wrote on October 25, 1918, that Hemingway had fallen in love with her. Despite being transferred to Florence, she wrote Ernest twenty times in three weeks, referring to Ernest as "the light of my existence." In one letter, she told Hemingway about a kitten she had rescued. "I wish you could have seen the thrilling rescue I just pulled off. A poor kitten was on the roof all night, & howling like mad. I found it when I came off duty & climbed up on a bench & window sill & got it down to the accompaniment of much grateful purring." Agnes knew Ernest would enjoy the story, as they were both fond of cats. By November 22, the couple was talking about marriage.

Agnes was seven and half years older than Ernest. Despite their age difference, the tall, slender woman with chestnut brown hair, lovely gray-blue eyes, and a flirtatious smile had captured Hemingway's heart. According to Henry S. Villard and James Nagel, in their biography, *Hemingway in Love and War: The Lost Diary of Agnes von Kurowsky,* ". . . she was physically attractive in every way, and . . . had a personality to match. She was intelligent and interested, nurturing, and supportive, with a sense of humor and a craving for adventure." The wartime romance lasted five months. December 9, 1918, was the last time they saw each other. Hemingway was shipped home January 21, 1919. He had hoped Agnes would soon follow. But, in March, Agnes wrote Ernest that her heart now belonged to someone else. Hemingway was devastated, became physically ill, and took to his bed. Again, it was his sisters and his beloved cats that helped console the heartbroken young man.

In June, Agnes wrote Ernest that her love affair had ended and she was considering coming back to the States in July. But Hemingway had moved on with his life and was no longer interested in the woman he would later immortalize in his novel *A Farewell to Arms,* a woman in his fiction he fondly called Cat.

Hemingway during the war years

Hadley Richardson and Ernest Hemingway on their wedding day

chapter 4

The First Mrs. Hemingway

My dearest Katherine Cat—

Selected letters

During the month of October, 1920, Ernest Hemingway was introduced to twenty-eight-year-old Hadley Richardson, a St. Louis native visiting mutual friends in Chicago. He was immediately attracted to the tall, shy girl with the beautiful auburn hair and would later tell his younger brother, Leicester, that during his first meeting with Hadley he knew this lovely girl was the woman he was going to marry.

Ernest had recently resigned as a writer for the *Cooperative Commonwealth,* a slick monthly magazine, and was now submitting articles to the *Toronto Star.* After their marriage, Hadley's small trust fund would have to cover the couple's living expenses for their immediate future.

Ernest and Hadley wed on September 3, 1921, at the small County Church at Horton Bay in Upper Michigan. Hadley's attendants were Helen Breaker, Ruth Bradfield, and Katy Smith, who had introduced Hadley to Ernest. Hemingway's best man was Bill Horne. Bill Smith (Katy's brother), Carl Edgar, Art Meyers, and Jack Pentecost served as ushers.

The couple was pleased that the weather was perfect for their wedding, warm with blue skies. The weather was so accommodating that the bride and groom went swimming before the service began. Hadley arrived at the church with her hair still damp.

The newlyweds honeymooned for two weeks at Windermere, on the shore of Walloon Lake, where Hemingway, as a teenager, used to read late into the night with the family cats by his side. He was pleased to learn that his new bride shared his fondness for his feline companions.

Top: The cottage at Walloon Lake
Middle: The Hemingway family: Clarence, Leicester, Sunny, Ursula, Ernest, Grace, Carol and Marcelline
Bottom: Hadley was as fond of cats as Ernest was.

13

Ernest and Hadley made plans to go to Paris.

chapter 5

Too Poor to Own a Cat

*We could not afford a dog nor
even a cat then, and the only cats I knew were in the
cafés or small restaurants or great cats that I admired in
concierges' windows.*

A Moveable Feast

Paris was a cold, wet city when Ernest Hemingway and his first wife, Hadley Richardson, arrived on December 20, 1921. Ernest was excited about their new surroundings and what his future as a writer would bring. He and Hadley had first considered Italy, but author and friend Sherwood Anderson had recommended France to the young writer, telling him that Paris was where art was taken seriously. Anderson provided letters of introduction and the Hemingways arrived during the Christmas holidays. Hadley was soon homesick for family and friends.

A cat in the rain

Ernest and Hadley found accommodations at L'Hôtel Jacob et d'Angleterre on the Left Bank, which attracted a creative assortment of musicians, dancers, actors, painters, writers, and poets. The hotel was located in walking distance of the Dôme and the Rotonde cafés where many of the artists congregated. It was here among his peers that Hemingway settled down to the serious job of writing.

The newlyweds rented a small two-room cold-water apartment at 79 rue Cardinal Lemoine. It was a fourth-story walk-up, located in a poor, rough, working-class neighborhood. Ernest began a daily writing routine, working in a rented room of an old hotel on the rue Mouffetard. Hemingway had heard that the French poet Paul Verlaine had written and died in the room twenty-five years earlier. Whether the story was true or not, this may have been the reason Hemingway rented the shabby space. Although the room was hard to heat, there was a lovely view of the Paris rooftops, where pigeons came to roost.

The *Toronto Star* had agreed to accept a series of "Letters from Europe," giving Hemingway his own byline. When Ernest was working, Hadley spent many lonely hours in their cramped apartment reading, writing letters, practicing on her rented upright piano, and she considered adopting a kitten for company. Ernest loved cats as much as she did, but told his wife they were too poor to own a cat. Their funds were limited, and he could not justify the added expense. These words came back to haunt

Hemingway when he noticed how depressed his wife was becoming. Hadley was thirty years old, almost eight years his senior, considerably older than most women in those days who planned to start a family. Ernest knew how much she wanted to have a child. But, for now, having children was out of the question, and so was owning a cat.

Hadley's unexpected pregnancy changed Ernest's plans for the future and, eventually, his thoughts on owning a pet. Ernest began work on a short story *Cat in the Rain,* about a lonely American woman who sees a kitten in the rain and tries to rescue it.

"I wanted it so much," she said, "I don't know why I wanted it so much. I wanted that poor kitty. It isn't any fun to be a poor kitty. It isn't any fun to be a poor kitty out in the rain."

The story was a tribute to Hadley, who was dealing with her first year of marriage, the loneliness it entailed, and her deep desire for motherhood.

According to biographer Gioia Diliberto, in her biography, *Hadley,* Hemingway based the story on an incident that happened in Rapallo in 1923. Hadley was two months pregnant when she found a kitten that had been hiding under a table in the rain.

"I want a cat," she said. "I want a cat. I want a cat now. If I can't have long hair or any fun I can have a cat."

During Hadley's last months of pregnancy in Paris, Ernest gave his wife a small dog with a curled tail that they christened Wax Puppy, a dog that captured the hearts of both Ernest and Hadley.

In the summer of 1923 Hemingway's first book, *Three Stories & Ten Poems,* was published by Contract Publishing. Six months later in February 1924, Ernest finished his short story *Cat in the Rain*—which is considered by

Hemingway in front of the Paris apartment building where he and Hadley lived

many critics as one of his best. The story was included in Ernest's second book, *In Our Time,* a collection of short stories which was first published in Paris in March, 1924, by Three Mountains Press. The book was dedicated to Hadley.

A Paris cat strolls past a Montmartre café. Sacré-Coeur can be seen in the background.

Hemingway with his son Bumby in their Paris apartment at 113, rue Notre-Dame-des-Champs

chapter 6

Paris and Feather Puss

When I got home and into the courtyard and upstairs and
saw my wife and my son and his cat F. Puss all of them
happy and a fire in the fireplace . . .

A Moveable Feast

The Hemingways were happy to head back to Paris
with their baby in the winter of 1924. They had missed
their intellectual and artistic friends while on a five-
month sojourn to Canada, but both Hadley and Ernest
had agreed their child should be born on the other side of
the Atlantic. On arriving in Toronto in September, 1923,
the Hemingways rented a room at the Selby Hotel on
Sherbourne Street. The hotel, once an elegant Victorian
mansion, had seen better days. Hadley hoped they would
soon find more suitable quarters. A few weeks later Ernest
found an apartment they could afford at 1599 Bathurst
Street. The apartment was only one room with a Murphy
bed, but there was a rocking chair and a large bathtub
with claw feet which pleased Hadley. There was also room
for her rented grand piano. But it was the apartment's
balcony, and a view of the countryside, that made Ernest
decide on signing a year's lease.

*Above: The survival rate of stray
cats and kittens in Canada,
according to Hemingway, was
not good.*
*Below: Small dogs with curled
tails reminded Hemingway of
his Paris dog, Wax Puppy.*

In Toronto, on October 10, 1923, Hadley gave birth
to a healthy baby boy, John Hadley Nicanor, whom they
nicknamed Mr. Bumby, and soon shortened to Bumby.
Ernest worked for the *Toronto Star* as a reporter, bringing in,
as he said, "a steady income." One of the things Ernest learned
while working for the newspaper in Toronto under the tutelage of Harry Hindmarsh, the
paper's assistant managing editor, was that he no longer wished to practice journalism. He
and Hadley agreed that when they returned to Paris, Ernest would concentrate on his own
writing, just as writer and friend Gertrude Stein had suggested.

The only negative aspect of their decision to move back to Paris was being forced to
leave their adopted kitten Feather Kcat behind with friends in Toronto, a city, Ernest
complained, where the Humane Society disposed of cats by the bagfuls. While in
Toronto, Ernest had been gone much of the time, on assignment for the newspaper.
During Hadley's pregnancy, the cat became her constant companion. The kitten, to
Hadley's dismay, was not litter box–trained and soon found a convenient area behind
the bathtub. Hemingway wrote his friend and poet, Ezra Pound, that he would have to
clean up the cat's *"merde"* with copies of the *Toronto Star.*

Before leaving Canada for their trip back to Paris, they received news that Wax Puppy, the adorable little dog Ernest had given Hadley a few months before they left Paris, had died. Friend and publisher Bill Bird had agreed to keep the little dog until their return, but the puppy had been diagnosed with an incurable disease and had to be put down by the veterinarian. The Hemingways would return to Paris without a single pet companion.

Ernest was attracted to Hadley's beautiful auburn hair.

Hadley's pregnancy had initially been a surprise to Ernest and may have been planned by her, hoping a baby would strengthen their marriage after a disastrous incident had threatened to tear them apart in December of 1922. Hadley, on a request from Ernest, had packed a small suitcase containing eleven short stories and an unfinished novel. She had also packed almost all copies and carbons of Ernest's entire work. Then, she took the train to Lausanne, Switzerland, where Ernest was covering the Peace Conference for the *Toronto Star*. After the conference, the couple had planned a two-week ski vacation. It was the Christmas holidays and Hadley had been deliriously happy. She left her seat on the train for only a few minutes and when she returned, she noticed the suitcase was missing. Ernest said it was not Hadley's fault that the suitcase had been stolen. He had consoled his hysterical wife, possibly calling her his favorite endearing nicknames, Kat and Feather Kitty. But Hadley had been overwhelmed with guilt and could not stop crying. Days later, Ernest's silence and dark moods confirmed Hadley's suspicions that her husband did indeed blame her for the loss of his manuscripts.

Hadley may have thought a baby would mend everything. A child could bind them forever and, if not, fearing Ernest might leave her, she would at least have someone to love. Two months after the loss of the manuscripts, while vacationing with Ernest in Rapallo, Italy, Hadley announced that she was two months pregnant. Ernest was shocked. He was only twenty-three years old and would later complain to friend Gertrude Stein that he was too young to be a father. Years later, Hadley would tell friend and biographer Alice Hunt Sokoloff that, at the time, she thought having a baby was a wonderful idea.

The Hemingways, now a family of three, found a cheap coldwater flat on the second floor of a building above a small sawmill and lumberyard at 113 rue Notre-Dame-des-Champs. The apartment was larger than their previous Paris dwelling, with a second bedroom Ernest could use as a study, and a dressing room that could serve as a nursery for their son, Bumby. Although the apartment had no electricity and was dark, dingy, and drafty, at least it was located in a better neighborhood. They were in walking distance of the metro station; Ezra Pound's studio; Sylvia Beach's bookstore, Shakespeare and Co.; the Luxembourg Gardens; and Gertrude Stein's impressive home. The only drawback was the sawmill and the lumberyard located below the apartment. The dust from the mill may have added to Hadley's constant bronchial infections. The noise forced Hemingway to find a quieter atmosphere in which to work, seeking refuge at nearby cafés where the local cats would congregate, looking for their next meal. Hemingway wrote about the Paris café cats in his memoir, *A Moveable Feast*.

The Paris cat had large yellow eyes.

Hadley's friend, Kitty Cannell, surprised the Hemingways one morning, arriving at their new apartment with a gift for their son, Bumby. The present was a gentle, loving cat with large yellow eyes. Ernest immediately christened the cat Feather Puss, which was shortened to F. Puss. Years later Ernest would be known for giving his cats elaborate names that were always shortened to nicknames that could easily be remembered. F. Puss became the fourth member of the Hemingway household. Ernest would write fondly about the cat in *A Moveable Feast*:

> There were no babysitters then and Bumby would stay happy in his tall cage bed with his big, loving cat named F. Puss. There were people who said that it was dangerous to leave the cat with a baby. The most ignorant and prejudiced said that a cat would suck a baby's breath and kill him. Others said that a cat would lie on a baby and the cat's weight would smother him. F. Puss lay beside Bumby in the tall cage bed and watched the door with his big yellow eyes, and would let no one come near him when we were out and Marie, the femme de ménage, had to be away. There was no need for babysitters. F. Puss was the babysitter.

Hadley and Bumby in their Paris apartment

Ernest seemed to be settling into family life with his wife, young son, and the cat, despite Ernest's earlier complaining of fatherhood and the restrictions he thought it would put on his writing.

> I woke early, boiled the rubber nipples and the bottles, made the formula, finished the bottling, gave Mr. Bumby a bottle and worked on the dining-room table before anyone but he, F. Puss, the cat, and I were awake. The two of them were good company and I worked better than I have ever done.
>
> —*A Moveable Feast*

1924 proved a productive year for Ernest. According to biographer Michael Reynolds in *Hemingway: The Paris Years* ". . . he had, in just five months, written ten new short stories and all but finished his first solid book."

Pauline and Ernest at San Sebastian, 1927

chapter 7

A Feather Kitty Never Dies

I just remembered all the things we'd ever done
and all the songs,
A feather kitty's talent lies
In scratching out the other's eyes.
A feather kitty never dies
Oh immortality.

Selected Letters

Feather Kitty was one of Hemingway's favorite nicknames for his first wife, Hadley Richardson, and Hadley may have felt like scratching out the eyes of her friend Pauline Pfeiffer who, in 1926, became "the other woman" in her husband's life. Instead, she begrudgingly backed away. Hadley's decision to divorce Hemingway after five years of marriage was not an easy one. She was still in love with him, and he with her. But Hadley no longer had the energy, or the inclination, to compete with Pauline, an attractive assistant editor to the Paris edition of *Vogue* and the daughter of wealthy parents from Piggott, Arkansas. Hemingway would write in *A Moveable Feast* about his dilemma of loving two women at the same time.

Pauline was immediately attracted to Hemingway, and Ernest could not resist her charm.

> To truly love two women at the same time truly love them, is the most destructive and terrible thing that can happen to a man. . . . you do things that are impossible and when you are with one you love her and with the other you love her and together you love them both.

Pauline Pfeiffer and her sister, Virginia (Jinny), arrived in Paris in the spring of 1925. Friends said that Pauline had come to Paris to find a husband, but the truth was it was the prestigious position at *Vogue* that brought her to the city. Also, she had ended her engagement to her cousin, Matthew Herald, a prominent lawyer. What better place than Paris to sort out her feelings. She was petite and stylish, the opposite of Hadley. Her dark hair and eyes gave her an exotic look. She was smart,

witty, well read, and had an uncanny knowledge of the literary world. Hemingway was captivated by the Arkansas visitor. Hadley's friend, Kitty Cannell, who had given Bumby his beloved cat, F. Puss, introduced the Pfeiffer sisters to the Hemingways and, as their friendships grew, so did Pauline's interest in Ernest Hemingway. Hadley told biographer Alice Hunt Sokoloff that Ernest was almost weak when somebody loved him. Pauline was madly in love with Hemingway, constantly praising him and his work—something Hadley seldom did anymore, preoccupied with their son and motherhood.

Hemingway's book, *The Torrents of Spring,* was rejected by his publisher. Pauline encouraged Ernest to move to Charles Scribner's Sons. Hemingway's friend, author F. Scott Fitzgerald, had recommended Ernest to his editor, Max Perkins, at Scribner's, saying Hemingway would have a brilliant future. Scribner's published the book in May, 1926, and five months later also published Hemingway's novel, *The Sun Also Rises.* The main character, an American journalist, Jake Barnes, is in love with the flamboyant Lady Brett Ashley. The character of Brett was based on Lady Duff Twysden, a beautiful blonde Englishwoman whom Hemingway had befriended in Paris, a woman he had become infatuated with during his marriage to Hadley. *"She was built with curves like the hull of a racing yacht and you missed none of it, . . ."* Hemingway wrote in *The Sun Also Rises.* But, as with his first true love, Agnes von Kurowsky, Duff, aged thirty-two, would also wound Hemingway's ego when she turned her interest towards someone else. Hemingway's portrait of Duff in his novel was not flattering.

During the divorce proceedings, Hadley, Bumby, and F. Puss moved to a more comfortable apartment. Hadley wanted to be closer to Bumby's godmothers, Gertrude Stein, and Stein's companion, Alice B. Toklas. Hemingway, racked with guilt over the impending divorce, gave all profits and royalties of *The Sun Also Rises* to Hadley and dedicated the book to Hadley and their son, John Hadley Nicanor.

Although divorced, Hemingway would continue to correspond with Hadley until the end of his life, immortalizing her, their son, and F. Puss in *A Moveable Feast.* In his letters to Hadley, he would reminisce about their past together. Like his childhood years in Upper Michigan, his years with Hadley proved to be some of the happiest times of his life.

Hadley was thirty-six years old when she divorced Hemingway. Instead of feeling sorry for herself, she felt liberated. Through friends she was introduced to journalist Paul Scott Mowrer. Paul had been a correspondent for the *Chicago Daily News* and the European head of its foreign service. He was a poet, a published author, and had won a Pulitzer Prize for his foreign correspondence writing. Their friendship developed into a love that would last a lifetime, a relationship Ernest would come to envy.

Hemingway married Pauline Pfeiffer in Paris on May 10, 1927, in L'Eglise de St. Honore d'Eylau, at 9, Place Victor Hugo. Pauline's sister, Jinny, of whom Ernest was quite fond, served as her attendant. The couple honeymooned in the picturesque fishing village of Le Grau-du-Roi, near Aigues-Mortes, located in the marshy flats at the mouth of the Rhone River. Here the couple took long walks on the unspoiled beaches, swam, fished, and sunbathed. Hemingway wrote well in these natural surroundings.

Pauline did not have an independent income like first wife Hadley, but because of family backing could offer Ernest a more comfortable lifestyle. Biographer Bernice

Kert wrote in *The Hemingway Women: Those Who Loved Him—the Wives and Others* ". . . to assume Ernest married her for her money, or that it was even a major factor, is to undervalue greatly Pauline's originality and depth. As much as anything, it was her conviction that they were kindred spirits, uniquely right for one another, that aroused him. She was the other half that would make him complete. She was one with him and would be for him in a way that no other woman could."

Hadley married Paul Mowrer on July 3, 1933. Ernest was happy for her, and he admired and respected Paul. Although Ernest was now married to Pauline, he would never forget his first Feather Kitty.

Hadley, Bumby, and Ernest during happier times

Ernest and Pauline in Key West with a new Ford Roadster, a gift from Pauline's uncle, Gus Pfeiffer, 1928

chapter 8

The Isle of Cats

In France they geld cats and do not geld the horses.
France was a long way off.

The Torrents of Spring

The Hemingways visited Key West for the first time in early April, 1928. The town was fondly called the Isle of Cats by some of the local cat fanciers because of the large population of cats and kittens that inhabited the island.

Ernest and his wife, Pauline, now seven months pregnant, spent six weeks on the subtropical island waiting for their new, yellow Ford Roadster to arrive, a gift from Pauline's wealthy uncle, Gus Pfeiffer.

Hemingway was impressed by the southernmost city with its New England–style architecture, the Cuban influences that reminded him of his beloved Spain, and the turquoise blue water teaming with fish. He was also intrigued by the dozens of friendly feral cats that inhabited Key West's public docks, bringing back fond memories of the cats he had owned.

Ernest and Pauline took rooms above the Trevor and Morris Ford Agency. The apartment, only a few blocks from the docks, was dark and shabby and may have reminded Hemingway of the Paris apartment he had once shared with first wife Hadley, his son Bumby, and his cat F. Puss.

Hemingway was working on his new novel, *A Farewell to Arms.* His collection of short stories, *Men Without Women,* was published in October, 1927. In Key West, Ernest wrote in the mornings and fished from the docks and bridges in the afternoons. Feral cats became his daytime companions and were given the discarded bait and leftover scraps from the fish Ernest caught

Above: Hemingway fishing off the docks in Key West
Below: Feral cats lived among the public docks.

and filleted.

Although Hemingway was writing well in this Florida paradise, it was decided that they would go to Kansas City, Missouri, for the birth. On June 28, after eighteen hours of hard labor, Pauline gave birth by caesarean section to a healthy nine-and-a-half-pound baby boy they named Patrick. Pauline's difficult delivery would have a lasting effect on Ernest, and was possibly the deciding factor on Hemingway's decision to have Catherine Barkley, the heroine in his novel, *A Farewell to Arms,* die after giving birth.

According to biographer Bernice Kert, in *The Hemingway Women: Those Who Loved Him—The Wives and Others,* Ernest's first true love, Agnes von Kurowsky, the nurse he had met and fallen in love with in Italy, became the prototype for the character, Catherine Barkley. Her name Catherine, and her nickname, Cat, in the novel, were names Ernest had given his first wife Hadley. Michael Reynolds wrote in *Hemingway: The Homecoming,* "Catherine was an amalgam of his first love Agnes Hannah von Kurowsky, with one part Hadley and two parts Pauline." Hemingway's use of feline names for women he knew meant he held them in high regard.

Polydactyl cats were not uncommon in Key West. The cats in Key West helped keep down the rat population.

The Hemingways, now a family of three, returned to Key West in November of 1928, renting a house at 100 South Street, in walking distance of one of the best swimming beaches on the island. It was here in this house in Key West that Hemingway would complete his novel about love and war, *A Farewell to Arms.*

Ernest had just settled into a comfortable writing routine when he had to leave by train to pick up Bumby, arriving in New York for the holidays. En route back to Florida on December 6, Ernest received the news that his father had committed suicide in Oak Park, Illinois. At age 57, Dr. Clarence Edmonds Hemingway, despondent over mounting debts, escalating diabetes, and painful angina pectoris, put a revolver to his head and pulled the trigger. After the funeral and back in Key West, the grief-ridden Hemingway buried himself in his work, writing six hours a day. His sister Sunny had traveled from Oak Park to help with the typing.

During times of stress, Hemingway had always found comfort in the companionship of his cats. A visit to one of Key West's many outdoor cafés may have inspired this passage from *A Farewell to Arms:*

> *A fat gray cat with a tail that lifted like a plume crossed the floor to our table and curved against my leg to purr each time she rubbed. I reached down and stroked her.*

By the end of January 1929, *A Farewell to Arms* had been completed. Ernest's editor Max Perkins came to Key West personally to pick up the manuscript, calling the book "magnificent."

In April, the Hemingways set sail for France. Ernest and Pauline would not return to Key West until February 1930, renting a house on Pearl Street for a brief stay. Four months later, the Hemingways drove north to Wyoming, seeking cooler weather. But Key West was always in Hemingway's thoughts. During the spring of 1931, the Hemingways returned to Key West for another brief stay, renting the Fanny Curry home at the corner of United and Whitehead Streets. Pauline was again pregnant. Eager to please her husband, she ignored her doctor's warnings about her health and her previous difficult delivery, knowing how desperately Ernest wanted a daughter. Hemingway grew up under the influence of a strong independent mother, Grace Hall, four sisters, Marcelline, Ursula, Sunny, and Carol, and a servant girl, Ruth Gordon, who was treated more like family than a servant. Ernest would be sixteen before his brother Leicester was born. Although considered a man's man, Ernest enjoyed the close companionship of women.

The Hemingways made plans to go to Europe in May, and Ernest assured his wife they would be back in America long before the birth of their second child. On a previous trip to Key West, Ernest and Pauline had looked at a two-story Spanish colonial stone house with wraparound balconies on Whitehead Street, across the street from the Key West Lighthouse. With one child, another on the way, and Ernest's son Bumby visiting on holidays, the Hemingways were looking for a permanent residence that they could call home. The house was spacious enough for their growing family and had a spare room above the carriage garage at the rear of the property that Ernest could use as a studio. Pauline's uncle, Gus Pfeiffer, purchased the house for his favorite niece and Ernest, of whom he had become quite fond.

Pauline gave birth to her second son, also by caesarean section, on November 12, 1931, again in Kansas City. The child had beautiful blue-black hair like his mother, and weighed a healthy nine pounds. The Hemingways named their son Gregory Hancock. Although Pauline felt she had disappointed her husband by not giving him the girl child he so desperately wanted, she decided a third pregnancy was out of the question due to the medical risks.

The Hemingways moved into their new Key West home December 19, 1931, just in time for the Christmas holidays. By January 1932, Ernest had completed *Death in the Afternoon,* his book on the pageantry of bullfighting, which he dedicated to his wife, Pauline. She did not share his passion for the sport, but her support of her husband was all-encompassing. Ernest's son Bumby would later write in his autobiography, *Misadventures of a Fly Fisherman: My Life With and Without Papa,* of his father's belief that bullfighting was more than a sport. "It was the mid-thirties . . . and we saw bullfights in many small and large places, mostly in Central Spain. The first place,

The quaint architecture of Key West appealed to Ernest and Pauline. The Whitehead house is shown in the foreground. There was an inside staircase from the second floor to the roof, where, according to Ernest's son Patrick, the Hemingway children enjoyed gazing at the stars.

The Hemingways' house at 907 Whitehead Street, Key West, Florida, was the first home Ernest ever owned. Ernest and Pauline's bedroom was on the second floor and offered a lovely view of the lighthouse.

though, was Pamplona. . . . I do remember liking the bullfights despite the blood and gore because Papa took the trouble to explain them well to me and to see that I knew the reason these various bloody stages were necessary in the progression of the ancient ritual sacrifice these fights truly represented."

Ernest Hemingway hired the son of a friend and local charter guide Gene Hamilton to rake leaves at his house on Whitehead Street under the supervision of his caretaker. In fact Gene had raked leaves in the yards of several rental houses in Key West where Hemingway had briefly lived. The caretaker for the White-head property was fond of fish. Each Saturday Gene arrived at Hemingway's house with a string of grunts for the caretaker and two lobsters for Hemingway. According to Gene the caretaker would clean the fish and give the scrapes to the cats which roamed Hemingway's property. Gene recalled how the cats would congregate around Hemingway's chair when he was reading on the veranda. According to Gene "some of the cat's feet had so many toes that the cats looked like they were walking on dog feet."

Neighborhood cats often visited the Heming-way house and its lush gardens.

Polydactyl cats were known to live next door, and today they inhabit the grounds.

Hemingway standing on the stairs to the studio above the coach house at Whitehead Street. He had a catwalk constructed from the second floor balcony of the house to his workroom.

chapter 9

Key West—The Cats Next Door

. . . four coons, a possum, 18 goldfish, three peacocks
and a yard with a fig tree . . .

Selected Letters

Despite popular belief, according to son Patrick, Ernest Hemingway did not own cats when he and his second wife, Pauline, and their two sons, Patrick and Gregory, lived in Key West at 907 Whitehead Street. According to an article written by Mark Burrell in the *Miami Herald* on August 21, 1994, Patrick Hemingway stated that even though his father was fond of cats, he did not possess a single cat in Key West. Patrick went on to tell a story of a neighbor's cat who appeared to be hurt, possibly hit by a car. The cat had dragged itself into Hemingway's yard. Ernest, on seeing the injured cat, decided to put it out of its misery. He shot the cat in the head and gave it to his yard man to bury. Somehow the cat survived, but was now missing an eye because of Hemingway's bullet. After the article appeared in the Miami newspaper, Burrell received a letter from a Key West resident backing up Patrick's story. The letter writer was Hemingway's former Key West neighbor and the owner of a cat crippled from birth that indeed had been shot by Hemingway, yet survived. The neighbor also said his family had several polydactyl cats, possibly some of the forebears of the cats in Key West now known as the famed "Hemingway cats."

Ernest Hemingway was not out of character when he shot the injured cat, hoping to end the animal's suffering. Years later, Hemingway would recall memories of seeing a cat lying dead on the side of the road in Cuba and fearing it was his beloved cat Boise. He felt so distraught

Above: An ornate urn sits above a urinal from Sloppy Joe's, creating a fountain that was used by Ernest and Pauline's peacocks and the neighborhood cats.
Below: A Key West cat enjoys a noonday nap.

Patrick Hemingway and his brother, Gregory, playing with two of the neighbor's kittens

over the cat's death he considered taking the dead animal back to his farm for a proper burial. So moved was Hemingway that he wrote about the incident in *Islands in the Stream:*

> *One time on the Central Highway he had seen a cat that had been hit by a car and the cat, fresh hit and dead, looked exactly like Boy. His back was black*

and his throat, chest, and four feet were white and there was the black mask across his face. He knew it couldn't be Boy because it was at least six miles from the farm; but it had made him feel sick inside and he had stopped the car and gone back and lifted the cat and made sure it was not Boy and then laid him by the side of the road so nothing else would run over him. The cat was in good condition so he knew he was some one's cat, and he left him by the road so they would find him and know about him rather than have to worry about him. Otherwise he would have taken the cat into the car and had him buried at the farm. That evening, coming back to the farm, the body of the cat was gone from where he had left him so he thought his people must have found him.

Most island communities have to deal with rodent problems and Key West was no exception. To keep the rat population under control, many of the island residents owned cats. Even though Hemingway had handyman Toby Bruce build a brick wall around his property for privacy, it did not keep out the rats nor stop the neighborhood

Above: Several children playing in front of the brick wall surrounding the Hemingway house. The wall did not stop the island's cats from visiting.
Right: Patrick and Gregory enjoyed the company of the neighbors' cats.

A front view of the Whitehead house

cats from visiting. The city also had its share of stray cats. No matter where you looked in Key West, it was not hard to spot a cat.

In an interview, Patrick Hemingway was asked about two photographs of Patrick and his brother Gregory as young children in Key West playing with two striped kittens. Patrick said he didn't remember the kittens, but Patrick's wife, Carol, said that it was quite possible they belonged to the neighbors. Another photograph shows Patrick and Gregory holding a white Persian cat in the backyard at their Key West house. Patrick said he recalled the cat, but could not remember its name or to whom it belonged. But he did have a humorous story to tell about the cat. He and his family had been visiting friends Jane and Grant Mason at their home in Cuba. Jane loved animals and owned a variety of pets, including a monkey, peacocks, flamingos, pigeons, doves, parrots, and several dogs and cats. Patrick noticed Jane had painted her white pigeons in pastel colors, using food coloring for paint. He thought this was such a wonderful idea that on returning home to Key West he painted the white cat the same colors, also with food coloring dye. He said his father became very angry when he saw what he had done to the cat. The Persian eventually licked off all the dye, with no harm to the cat.

Another Key West photograph, taken in 1940 after Hemingway had moved to Cuba and that has appeared in several Hemingway biographies, shows Pauline and friends relaxing near the pool of the Whitehead Street house. In the foreground is a cat that may have been one of the many strays hoping to take up residence with the Hemingways, in the house Ernest once referred to as "grand." Eventually the Hemingway house would become a haven for Key West cats, possibly related to the polydactyl cats that befriended Ernest Hemingway while he worked, giving him, as he said, "valuable aid."

One of the polydactyl cats that inhabit the grounds.

Captain Stanley Dexter, a Key West boat captain, according to his granddaughter, presented Hemingway with a white, polydactyl cat named Snowball when Ernest lived on Whitehead Street. Local boat captains believed that cats with extra toes brought the owner good luck. Years later in Cuba another boat captain would give Hemingway a cat as a gift, an Angora tiger which Ernest named Good Will.

Patrick and Gregory in Key West. They painted the cat with food coloring, which the cat eventually licked off.

It was not hard to spot a cat in Key West. A local feline greets visitors at the popular restaurant and historic site My Blue Heaven where Hemingway once boxed.

chapter 10

Not a Cat Fancier

Since I've spent so much time with my cats and seen
everything they have to go through, I don't mind so
much never having had a daughter.

Selected Letters

It is clear from Hemingway's work in his novel *Islands in the Stream* that his cats represented loyalty and devotion to him. So, it is not surprising that three of his four wives were fondly referred to either as Kat, Kath, Cat, Feather Kitty, Katherine Cat, Kitten, or Kittner. Pauline would be the only wife who would not claim this distinction. Perhaps it was because she did not share the same affection toward cats as did Hemingway and his other wives.

Ernest and Pauline had been married nine years when Hemingway met twenty-eight-year-old Martha Gellhorn at Sloppy Joe's Bar in Key West. He set aside working on his book, *To Have and Have Not,* a novel of rum-running between Cuba and Key West in the 1930s, to entertain the beautiful young woman. Her visit was short, but by the time she left the island Gellhorn, who was also a writer, had captured Hemingway's heart. Friend and author Malcolm

Martha Gellhorn captured Hemingway's heart in December, 1936.

Cowley fondly remembered Martha in his book *The Dream of the Golden Mountains: Remembering the 30s* as a "Bryn Mawr girl with literary ambitions and a lot of yellow hair."

Hemingway was thirty-seven years old when he became infatuated with Gellhorn. His marriage to Pauline was already showing signs of serious trouble. The passion he

Pauline was no match for Martha

Jane Kendall Mason was considered an international beauty.

had once felt for the woman he had fondly called Pilar was now gone. Also, after two difficult births, Pauline's doctors had recommended she not get pregnant again, dashing Ernest's hopes of ever having a daughter. Hemingway had first turned his affections toward Jane Kendall Mason, the beautiful, unhappily married, strawberry-blonde socialite who lived in Cuba and whom Hemingway may have thought young and healthy enough to bear him more children. Hemingway first met Jane, an athletic twenty-two-year-old with a wild streak, aboard the *Ile de France* in 1931 when they were both on a return trip to the United States. Jane, like Pauline, had fallen under the spell of the handsome writer. According to Michael Reynolds in his biography *Hemingway: the 1930s,* "The face of Jane Mason was a study in white and gold, a face to turn any

Hemingway's favorite bar in Key West was Sloppy Joe's, owned by his good friend Joe Russell. It was rumored that Hemingway gave Russell the money to buy the bar and was a silent partner, although no papers were ever signed to make the transaction legal.

man's head. . . . she was the young beauty whose wild streak added to her excitement. Tallish, big boned and athletic, she wanted all her life to be remembered for something more than her beautiful face. . . . she was an active sportswoman and sometime daredevil, danced so well the floor cleared to watch her, at one time owned and managed a Havana art gallery [she was a talented sculptor and painter] and was fluent in three languages." It was easy to understand Hemingway's attraction to the beautiful adventurer. But their five-year relationship ended badly in April 1936 when Jane, like Hemingway's past love interests Agnes Von Kurowsky and Lady Duff Twysden, turned her affections toward someone else. Hemingway would remember Jane in his fiction, as he had done with other women he had loved. But his portrait of the blonde, blue-eyed beauty as the wealthy, beautiful, and married Mrs. Helen Bradley in his novel *To Have and Have Not* would not be kind. Nevertheless, years later, Mason would tell biographer Bernice Kert in *The Hemingway Women*, "If we had not been married to other people we would have probably married."

Martha Gellhorn, like her new lover, was fond of nicknames, calling him Ernestino, Bug, or Big Kitten. When she was angry with Ernest, she called him The Pig.

Martha had recently ended an affair with a married man, French journalist Bertrand de Jouvenel. According to biographer Carl Rollyson in his book *Nothing Ever Happens to the Brave: The Story of Martha Gellhorn,* Bertrand walked out on his wife to travel with Martha throughout Europe. Gellhorn knew how to play the game of mistress, and she played it well. Pauline never had a chance to save her marriage.

In January 1937 Hemingway made plans to go to Spain to cover the Spanish Civil War as an anti-war correspondent for the North American Newspaper Alliance. According to Carlos Baker in *Ernest Hemingway: A Life Story,* ". . . he said it was his purpose to make America aware of the new kind of war now being waged by Franco and his foreign allies. It was a total war, said he [Hemingway], in which there was no such thing as a noncombatant." Hemingway set sail February 27 aboard the S.S. *Paris.*

Hemingway's new love, Martha Gellhorn, would meet him in the war-torn city of Madrid. She was covering the war for Colliers. According to Christopher Ondaatje, in his biography *Hemingway in Africa: The Last Safari,* "The affair between her and Hemingway blossomed in the Spanish War. . . . free of all responsibilities, amid the falling shells and fighting, with the prospect of imminent death charging the present with excitement, Hemingway and Gellhorn fell in love." Hemingway returned to Key West at the end of May. His life with Pauline would never be the same. Hemingway still loved Pauline, but as had happened when married to his first wife, he found himself once more in love with two women. Unfortunately for Ernest, Pauline would not be as complacent about divorcing her husband as Hadley had been.

By 1939, Key West no longer offered Hemingway the solitude he needed to work on his new novel *For Whom the Bell Tolls,* a book he felt would become one of his greatest works. Good friend Sara Murphy, recovering from recent surgery, informed him that she would be arriving in Key West for a visit. He would stay long enough to see his "dearest Sara." Ernest had first met Sara and her husband, Gerald, in Paris in 1925 when he was married to Hadley. According to Amanda Vaill in her biography of the Murphys: "[Sara] adored Hemingway from the outset. His artistic sensibility, . . . his macho swagger—tempered disarmingly by his occasionally self-deprecating grin— . . . struck her most." Hemingway was also fond of the beautiful and aristocratic woman with the dark gold-blonde hair and slanted blue eyes whom friend and writer F. Scott Fitzgerald referred to as the "Viking Madonna."

Sara Sherman Wiborg Murphy was sixteen years Hemingway's senior, but her elfin personality, delicate features, and youthful spirit made Sara appear much younger than her years. It was said that Ernest had a crush on this independently wealthy, well-traveled, well-read beauty with a serious interest in art. Ripe for adventure, she was once described as "a cat who goes her own way." Sara was also one of the few women Ernest knew, except for Jane Mason, who felt comfortable on a boat and loved to fish. In a letter to Sara in 1939 after their visit in Key West, Hemingway wrote that he had visited the cove where they had picnicked.

> *I never could thank you for how loyal and lovely and also beautiful and attractive—you have always been since always. . . . I wish we were killing the rainy afternoons together. It is a beautiful storm. I love you always and please always count on it.*

Sara, with her quiet, intelligent charm, had captured Hemingway's heart in a way few women would, although they apparently never acted on their feelings for one another. Hemingway adored Sara, but he never quite warmed to Gerald, despite Gerald's deep devotion to his children, family, friends, and pets—Gerald and Sara even celebrated their dog's birthdays. Years later Ernest would write friend and poet

Archibald MacLeish describing his feelings for Sara's husband.

> *I like Gerald . . . but always felt about him the way people who do not like cats feel about cats. But . . . I love Sara.*

But it was Martha Gellhorn who would become the next Mrs. Hemingway. In April of that year Hemingway left for Cuba to start a new life with Martha, a woman he hoped would give him the girl child he so desperately wanted. Unknown to Hemingway Martha had an abortion in 1931. Ernest would soon learn motherhood for Martha was not a priority.

Pauline divorced Ernest on November 4, 1940, after a bitter separation. The divorce was uncontested, giving Pauline custody of their two sons, Patrick and Gregory. According to biographer Michael Reynolds, thirteen years of marriage had produced seven books, making Hemingway's life in Key West with Pauline the most prolific time of his life.

Pauline, left behind, continued to live in Key West and would tell Ernest's sister, Marcelline, in 1950 that she never stopped loving Ernest.

A Key West cat enjoys the lush foliage of the Hemingway garden below the tree.

A strangler fig tree planted by Hemingway grew into an impressive tree, and a favorite place for cats to hunt lizards. Years later the tree was toppled by hurricane winds.

Martha Gellhorn, the first mistress of the Finca Vigia, on the front steps of the house with her favorite cat, Thruster

One of the Finca's stray cats

chapter II

The Stray Cats of Finca Vigia

"Bring me a whiskey with mineral water," Thomas
Hudson said. "And bring milk for the cats. . . ."
Islands in the Stream

Hemingway wanted to please the new woman
in his life, Martha Gellhorn, whom he fondly
called Marty, Mook, or Kitten. He assured her that
the small hotel room at the Ambos Mundos in
downtown Havana was only temporary until they
found a suitable house. Martha heard about an
aging estate for rent, Finca Vigia (Lookout Farm),
in the village of San Francisco de Paula. Gellhorn,
an avid tennis player, was pleased to find the farm
not only had a spacious house where she and Ernest
could write, but also had a large pool and a tennis
court. Ernest enjoyed the game of tennis, despite
the 1918 war wounds to his legs that limited his
skills in some of his favorite sports, such as tennis
and boxing.

The grounds of the farm were unkempt, and a large
grove of mango trees laden with ripe fruit had attracted
a significant number of fruit rats. The rats had in turn

*The ripe fruit of the mango grove at-
tracted rats, which attracted the area's
cats.*

attracted visits by the area's cats. The abandoned outbuildings of the farm made desirable homes
for a number of strays. Martha, a cat fancier like Ernest, knew the value of these feline hunters.
Not only would the stray cats keep the rat population under control, but she may have felt Ernest's
fondness for his feline friends might be the deciding factor on getting Hemingway to agree to rent
the estate despite its rundown appearance. Whether due to the noticeable improvements Martha
had already made to the property with her own money, or the stray cat population entrenched on
the grounds of the Finca, Hemingway agreed to move into the "joint on the top of a hill," as he
described the home to his editor, Max Perkins. Hemingway wrote well in his new home, according
to Carlos Baker in his biography *Ernest Hemingway: A Life Story,* ". . . at the rate of 700 to 1000
words a day. He said that he was so happy with his work that it was sometimes 7:30 in the evening
before he remembered to drink his usual three scotches before dinner."

Ernest and Martha were married November 20, 1940, in Cheyenne, Wyoming, by
a justice of the peace. They honeymooned in New York at the Hotel Barclay, but left
in time to spend Christmas at their Cuban home with close friends and their newly
acquired stray cats. Hemingway purchased the farm December 28, 1940, with the
proceeds from his novel *For Whom the Bell Tolls,* which he had dedicated to his new
love, Martha Gellhorn.

Hemingway gives a gentle scratch to Uncle Wolfer, the son of Princessa, who was the grandmother of all Finca cats.

chapter 12

Hemingway's Dearest Cat Friends

*Princessa was a delicate and aristocratic cat . . . with
beautiful manners. . . .*

Selected Letters

As a child, Hemingway loved reading about the ancient battles of the Egyptians. He was aware that the ancient Egyptians were worshippers of the cat, believing that cats brought prosperity and good fortune to those who owned them. He also may have read that the cat was considered to be a talisman of fertility by the ancient Egyptians.

Whether it was Martha's lack of interest in motherhood or the loneliness Hemingway experienced while his wife was away on writing assignments, Ernest decided to purchase a cat, apparently not satisfied with the legions of outdoor strays around him at the Finca. He purchased a young, purebred, female Persian from the Silver Dawn Cattery in Miami, Florida. According to Dr. Marty Becker in *The Healing Power of Pets,* "pets motivate people to fight depression." Hemingway suffered from severe bouts of loneliness and depression when Martha was away. He may have thought a cat would be good company, remembering the cats who had been his companions in his childhood and most of his adult life.

A Persian is a breed known to be docile, quiet, intelligent, aloof, gentle, easy-going, good-tempered, sweet-natured, affectionate, and friendly, according to zoologist and cat expert Desmond Morris in *Cat World: A Feline Encyclopedia.* These were the traits Hemingway, as a writer, was looking for in a cat—traits similar to the personality of F. Puss, his Paris cat. He said that he wrote well there in the early part of the day with F. Puss and his son, Bumby, by his side.

Hemingway's Cuban home became a haven for stray cats and dogs.

Hemingway's new Persian, Princessa, turned out to be an affectionate cat, just as he had hoped. He and Martha christened her Tester (aka Baby) but the Finca staff felt she deserved a much more aristocratic name because of her elegant ways and renamed her Princessa, which, Hemingway agreed, fit her perfectly. Ernest would reminisce about his loving cat in *Islands in the Stream:*

Patrick, Ernest, and Gregory enjoyed time with their cats Good Will, Princessa, and Boise.

> *Princessa was such a delicate and aristocratic cat, smoke gray, with golden eyes and beautiful manners, and such a great dignity that her periods of being in heat were like an introduction to, and an explanation and finally exposition of, all the scandals of royal houses. Since he had seen Princessa in heat, not the first tragic time, but after she was grown and beautiful, and so suddenly changed from all her dignity and poise into wantonness, Thomas Hudson knew that he did not want to die without having made love to a princess as lovely as Princessa.*

Princessa adored Hemingway and would rise when he did at first light, stretching out on Ernest's desk, patiently watching him work, or napping while he wrote, and giving him as he said "valuable aid." Soon after Princessa arrived at the Finca, Hemingway adopted a half-Maltese kitten named Willy (aka Willie, Mr. Willy, or Uncle Willy) to keep Princessa company. Willy was a beautiful gray-and-black-striped cat with silky fur, a favorite of his sons Patrick and Gregory. He was known for his loud purr purr (Hemingway's language) and gentle nature and had acquired a taste for Hemingway's home-grown catnip which made him purr even louder. Willy was definitely a people cat and loved to be picked up and have his stomach stroked. He was especially fond of Hemingway and would keep him company while he wrote. Ernest would write about the gentle, loving cat in *Islands in the Stream:*

> *I'll get catnip in town if there is any and get Goats and Willy and Boy drunk tonight on it. There still should be some catnip in the shelf of drawers in the cat room if it hasn't gotten too dry and lost its force. It lost its force very quickly in the tropics and the catnip that you raised in the garden had no force at all. I wish we non-cats had something that was as harmless as catnip that would have as much effect, he thought. Why don't we have something like that we can get drunk on?*

Hemingway considered purchasing a purebred Persian male to mate with Princessa but then reconsidered. Ernest had been fascinated with the idea of starting a new breed of cat, possibly with an Angora. Angora cats were known to be alert, intelligent, loyal, gentle-natured, and to respond well to play. Several of Hemingway's cat books in his Finca library had chapters on the unusual breed. Ernest also considered a Cuban cat as a possible suitor for Princessa. Despite the harsh living conditions of the Cuban strays in the nearby village, the Cuban cats seemed to be flourishing.

Boise had the run of the house.

An energetic kitten soon caught the attention of Hemingway. A Cuban kitten with unusual black and white markings was playing with its own reflection on the glass cigar counter of the La Terraza Restaurant and Bar in the fishing village of Cojimar when Ernest noticed him. It was Christmas morning and the bar was relatively quiet except for a few villagers who were still recuperating from the holiday parties the night before. The restaurant was a popular gathering place for the local fishermen.

Hemingway already owned two cats, his elegant Persian, Princessa, and the good-natured kitten named Willy. But Hemingway knew Princessa would soon be going into her first heat, and Ernest was worried that the stray cats from the neighborhood were already starting to notice her.

The proprietor of the restaurant brought out a plate of freshly cooked prawns for Hemingway and his youngest son Gregory, who, with older brother Patrick, was visiting Ernest and Martha for the holidays. Ernest broke off a small piece of the prawn and fed it to the kitten, who attacked it hungrily. Hemingway would immortalize the kitten in his novel *Islands in the Stream*:

> *Thomas Hudson looked at the kitten, with his handsome black and white markings, his white chest and forelegs and the black, like a formal mask across his eyes and forehead, eating the prawn and growling, and asked the proprietor who he belonged to.*
> *"You if you want him."*
> *"I have two at the house, Persians."*
> *"Two is nothing. Take this one. Give them a little Cojimar blood."*

Patrick and Boise

Hemingway's son, Gregory, urged his father to take the cat.

> *"Papa, can't we have him? Please, Papa, can't we have him? He's a beautiful cat.*
> *"Do you think he'd be happy away from the sea?"*
> *"Certainly, papa. He'll be miserable here in a little while. Haven't you seen how miserable the cats are in the streets? And they were probably just like him once."*
> *"Take him," the proprietor said. "He'll be happy on a farm."*

The adopted stray kitten was christened Dillinger (aka Dingie, Boy, Boysy, Boissy D'Angelas) and was later changed to Boise. The young Cuban cat became the third feline to join the Finca's principal cat colony and would become Ernest's dearest and closest cat friend, whom he would come to call Brother.

Soon after Boise was brought home to the farm, Good Will (aka Willy), named in honor of Nelson Rockefeller, joined the clan. Good Will was a beautiful Angora tiger cat from Guanabacoa and was given to Hemingway as a Christmas present by a local fisherman. Hemingway would write about this transaction in *Islands in the Stream*:

> *"Listen, Tomás," one of the fisherman who had been listening to the conversation from the table said. "If you want cats I can get an Angora, a genuine Angora, from Guanabacoa. A true Tiger Angora."*
> *"Male?"*
> *"As much as you," the fisherman said. At the table they all laughed. . . . "Listen, Tomás. Do you want the Angora Tiger from Guanabacoa?" the fisherman asked.*
> *"What is he? A witchcraft cat?"*
> *"Witchcraft nothing. This cat never even heard of Saint Barbara. This cat is more of a Christian than you are."*
> *"Es muy posible," another fisherman said and they all laughed.*
> *"What does this famous beast cost?" Thomas Hudson asked.*

Gregory, Hemingway's youngest son, urged his father to adopt Boise. Hemingway wrote about this incident in his novel Islands in the Stream.

"*Nothing. He's a gift. A genuine Angora Tiger. He's a Christmas gift.*"

Good Will was a gentle, loving cat and enjoyed the attention he received from Ernest and Martha. He had the run of the house, napping in Ernest's favorite living room chair when vacant, where he graciously posed for photographs. Hemingway, an accomplished photographer, enjoyed taking pictures of family, friends, and his cats. Although Good Will had a pleasing personality, Boise remained Hemingway's favorite.

As Boise grew into an adult cat he became Hemingway's constant companion. He joined Princessa and Willy in the early morning hours, keeping Hemingway company while he worked. Boise would patiently sit on the bookcase while Ernest wrote, catnap on Ernest's desk, or sun himself on the windowsill nearby. Boise took daily strolls throughout the grounds with Ernest, wanting to be with him as much as possible, knowing it was just a matter of time before Hemingway would leave on his next trip. Hemingway captured one of these moments in *Islands in the Stream:*

> Boise was following him, a little worried at
> this going away but not panicking since there

Patrick and Gregory playing with Boise, who was adopted from Cojimar

Ernest and Boise on the front terrace of the Finca

Hemingway with his closest cat friend, Boise

was no baggage and no packing.

Boise was welcome at every meal, sitting on the dining room table and being hand fed by Hemingway. Ernest said that Boise was the world's most sophisticated cat in his food preference, dining on such delicacies as freshly cut mangos, chili con carne, chop suey, coleslaw, and all pies and cakes. Hemingway wrote to his family and friends about his unique cat and immortalized Boise in *Islands in the Stream,* devoting thirty-five pages to his beloved cat.

> . . . *he ate everything the man ate especially all those things that cats would not touch. Thomas Hudson remembered the summer before when they had been eating breakfast together and he had offered Boise a slice of fresh, chilled mangoes. Boise had eaten it with delight and he had mango every morning as long as Thomas Hudson was ashore and the mango season lasted. He had to hold the slices for him so he could get them into his mouth since they were slippery for the cat to pick off the plate and he thought he must rig some sort of rack, so the cat could take them without having to hurry.*

Good Will, the Angora tiger cat, enjoyed relaxing and posing for photographs in Hemingway's living room chair.

According to Hemingway, Boise and Princessa wasted no time in mating, and thus began the Finca Vigia cat dynasty. Their first litter included five healthy kittens which Hemingway and Martha joyfully christened Friendless, Friendless's Brother, Thruster, Furhouse, and Fatso. To celebrate the occasion the kittens were served saucers of warm milk.

Boise would join Hemingway in the Finca's dining room for most meals.

Hemingway and his dog Negrita enjoy a quiet moment by the pool. A large scar on Hemingway's forehead, from an accident caused by a falling skylight in Paris in 1928, was still prominent years later.

chapter 13

Negrita Finds a Home

... her tail curled over her back,
her tiny feet and delicate legs
almost sparkling ... her eyes
loving and intelligent ...

Islands in the Stream

It was not unusual for Ernest Hemingway and Martha Gellhorn to see stray, hungry cats and dogs scouring the dumps and garbage cans of Havana and the outlying villages for scraps of food. It is still the same today. Now most of the strays are the offspring of those abandoned by Cubans who left their pets behind when they sought asylum in the United States. Many of the abandoned dogs are small in size, either white, short-haired dogs with brown or black spots, or longer-haired dogs with thick curly coats that shade their eyes. Feeding a pet in Cuba, whether it is a cat or dog, has often been considered a luxury. As it was

A Cuban fisherman with his dog

when food was limited under dictator Fulgencio Batista's corrupt reign—and as it is now due to the United States' continued embargo of over forty-five years against Cuba, many families struggle to feed themselves. Although a monthly government allotment of food guarantees that no one in Cuba will ever go hungry, there is, of course, no food allotment for pets. During some of the most severe economic times—after Russia discontinued their economic support to Cuba, and during the strict enforcement of the United States' embargo against the small island nation and its people—it was not unheard of for Cubans to butcher homeless cats or dogs roaming the countryside and cities to provide added meat for their families.

Hemingway captures in *Islands in the Stream* the plight of two poor elderly Cubans and their dog whom he and Martha Gellhorn had seen on several occasions during their trips to Havana in the early 1940s. Ernest also added just a glimpse of his wife's independent nature. It would not be until Fidel Castro took control of the government that the shanty

57

Abandoned dogs in Havana. These dogs struggle to survive, scrounging for food on the city streets.

towns would be bulldozed and the poor moved to better quarters in the cities.

> *He had looked at the old couple that lived in the board and palm frond lean-to they had built against the wall that separated the railway track from the a tract of ground where the electric company stored coal they unloaded from the harbor. The wall was black with coal dust from the coal that was hauled overhead on the unloader and it was less than four feet from the roadbed of the railway. The lean-to was built at a steep slant and there was barely room for two people to lie down in it. The couple who lived in it were sitting in the entrance cooking coffee in a tin can. They were Negroes, filthy, scaly with age and dirt, wearing clothes made from old sugar sacks, and they were very old. He could not see the dog.*
>
> *"Y el perro?" he asked the chauffeur.*
>
> *"Since a long time I haven't seen him."*
>
> *They had passed these people now for several years. At one time the girl whose letters he had read last night, had exclaimed about the shame of it each time they had passed the lean-to.*
>
> *"Why don't you do something about it, then?" he had asked her. "Why do you always say things are so terrible and write so well about how terrible they are and never do anything about it?"*
>
> *This made the girl angry and she had stopped the car, gotten out, gone over to the lean-to and given the old woman twenty dollars and told her this was to help her find a better place to live and to buy something to eat.*
>
> *"Sí señorita," the old woman said. "You are very amiable."*
>
> *The next time they came by the couple were living in the same place and waved happily. They had bought a dog. It was a white dog too, small and curly, probably not bred originally, Thomas Hudson thought, for the coal dust trade.*
>
> *"What do you think has become of the dog?" Thomas Hudson asked the chauffeur.*
>
> *"It probably died. They had nothing to eat."*
>
> *"We must get them another dog," Thomas Hudson said.*

A homeless puppy in Cojimar

On occasion, Ernest would see stray dogs congregating outside his favorite bar in Havana, the Floridita. The smells from the kitchen attracted both cats and dogs to the area. Hemingway had already adopted several small mixed-breed dogs with curled tails from his village, calling them his Cuban mongrels. One evening outside the Floridita a female dog caught his attention. She wasn't young, but her demure and curled tail reminded him of the dog he had given his first wife, Hadley, in Paris during her last months of pregnancy, a dog they had named Wax Puppy. Hemingway was captivated by the stray dog's personality, just as he had been by that of his Cuban kitten, Boise, whom he had recently adopted from Cojimar. He took the little dog home, named her Negrita, and would later write about her in *Islands in the Stream*:

> Thomas Hudson handed the drink to the chauffeur to hold and stooped to pet the dogs. Boise was sitting on the steps, watching them with contempt. There was Negrita, a small black bitch going gray with age, her tail curled over her back, her tiny feet and delicate legs almost sparkling as she played, her muzzle as sharp as a fox terrier and her eyes loving and intelligent. He had seen her one night in a bar following some people out and asked what breed of dog she was.

> "Cuban," the waiter had said. "She has been here four days. She follows everyone out but they always shut the doors of their cars on her."

> They had taken her home to the Finca and for two years she had not been in heat and Thomas Hudson had thought she was too old to breed. Then, one day, he had to break her loose from a police dog and after that she had police dog pups, pups from a pit bull, pointer pups, and a wonderful unknown pup that was bright red and looked as though his father might have been an Irish setter except that he had the chest and shoulders of a pit bull and a tail that curled up over his back like Negrita's.

> Now her sons were all around her and she was pregnant again. "Who did she breed with? Thomas Hudson asked the chauffeur. "I don't know."

> Mario, who came out with a sweater and gave it to the chauffeur, who took off his frayed uniform coat to put it on, said, "The father is the fighting dog in the village."

> "Well, goodbye dogs," Thomas Hudson said. "So long, Boy," he said to the cat who came bounding down through the dogs to the car. Thomas Hudson, sitting in the car now, holding a cork-wrapped drink, leaned out of the window and touched

A Cuban pointer from the village

the cat who rose on his hind legs to push his head against his fingers. "Don't worry, Boy. I'll be back."

"Poor Boise," Mario said. He picked him up and held him in his arms and the cat looked after the car as it turned, circling in the flower bed, and went down the uneven gully-washed driveway until it was hidden by the hill slope and tall mango trees. Then Mario took the cat into the house and put him down and the cat jumped up onto the window sill and continued to look out at where the driveway disappeared under the hill.

Mario stroked him but the cat did not relax.

"Poor Boise," the tall Negro boy said. "Poor, poor Boise."

Ernest enjoyed the companionship of the ever-growing family of cats and dogs, but they did not replace the enjoyment he felt when his three sons would visit. In a letter written to Pauline on July 19, 1941, he wrote about their two sons. He missed the boys

Hemingway missed his sons when they weren't with him.

terribly and was looking forward to their visit. He wished Pauline a happy birthday and told her of the arrangements he was making to have his sons picked up for their vacation in Idaho by friend Toby Bruce. He closed the letter with a mention of a man they both knew who had lost his boat in a storm.

> *Bought skiff with the $60 for that old man on the waterfront we called "Langosta" who with his dog, has been starving to death since he lost his [skiff].*

Throughout his life, Hemingway, like his father Clarence and Grandfather Hall before him, would continue to help those in need—people and beasts—despite his reputation as a selfish bully, a myth he helped to create.

On July 23, 1942, Hemingway wrote first wife Hadley. Alone at the Finca, he remembered back to happier times and shared news with her about his Cuban cats.

> *Dearest Kat,*
>
> *. . . We have three good cats here so I sang them the song and they were very pleased.*
>
> *We have a genuine Wax Puppy too with a tail curled exactly the same way and the cats all like him. The cats are a smoke grey Persian called "Tester" [Princessa]*

Sons Patrick, John, and Gregory enjoyed their vacations with their father.

and a black and white cat called Dillinger [Boise]or Boissy D'Anglas and a half maltese cat called Willy who is just a kitten and has a huge purr-prr. When I can't sleep at night I tell them stories about F. Puss and our great cat Mooky out west who fought the badger. When I say "THE BADGER!" Tester has to get under the sheets she is so frightened.

Good bye Miss Katherine Kat. I love you very much. It is all right to do so because it hasn't anything to do with you and that great Paul, it is just untransferable feeling for early and best Gods. But will never mention it if bad. Thought you might just be interested to know.

When corresponding with his sons, Ernest would include the updates of the recent births and deaths of his beloved pets. In a letter to his son Patrick, written on October 7, 1942, he shared his sorrow on the death of a cat and his concern about how his youngest son Gigi [Gregory] was dealing with the cat's demise.

Dearest Mousie:

We were awfully glad to get your letter. . . . Gigi wrote you about the poor Bates dying. It was really awful. He had that same thing that killed Pony, that took so long for him to die, but we gave him all the medicine he should have had and took good care of him and did everything we could about it. But Gigi felt awful about it and we didn't know how he would stand up under it finally. He took it very well really because he has such a good sense and though he loved Bates he knew there was nothing we could do about it. The other thing that helped him out is that Wolfer had got to be such a fine cat and that we have Testor's new baby who is a wonder cat.

He looks just like Boysy except that he is a Persian and has long fur and he is as strong as a bear and is built like a wolverine. Testor is lovely with him and takes such good care of him and has purred almost every minute since he has been born. He is three weeks old yesterday and is now able to make a purr-purr and to walk around and is really a marvelous cat. . . .

Boysy is in fine shape and so is Willy and so is the new cat and Stoopy Wolfer. I found that what was the matter with your catnip was that you planted it too shallow. You need to drill down the holes and plant it deep because what was coming up as long stalks with you was really the roots of the plant. Once you planted it deep enough the leaves had a chance to develop.

By 1943, Hemingway, with Martha away on assignment, found the loneliness in his Cuban home almost too much to bear. He wrote often to his sons and shared news about the cats. Ernest wrote his son Patrick, October 30, 1943. Martha had been gone five days.

Old Moose I certainly miss you. It is lonesomer than limbo here. Only the cotsies for company. Your Will as fine as ever. Boisie very loving and good. Friendless has gotten to be a great cat. Thruster mean and distant. Tester nice with me but mean with everybody else. Furhouse and Bro fine. Fats is as big as a skunk and moves the same way. He is a fine slow friendly good cat.

Hemingway often shared the news of his pets in letters not only to his sons and wives, but also in letters to close friends who he knew also shared a fondness for animals or owned cats and dogs themselves.

Hemingway's cats enjoyed doing tricks for their master. Littless Kitty preferred to watch.

chapter 14

The Circus Cats

The early morning breeze . . . was . . . stirring his dark
mane, and the lion looked huge, silhouetted on the rise
of the bank in the gray morning light, his shoulders
heavy, his barrel of a body bulking smoothly.

*The Short Happy Life
of Francis Macomber*

When Hemingway found himself at home alone
in Cuba, which was often the case in the early 1940s
while Martha Gellhorn was away on assignment as
a war correspondent, Hemingway would often pass
the time teaching his cats circus tricks on the front
terrace of his home, Finca Vigia. Hemingway wrote
his son Patrick October 30, 1943, sharing news
about his cats and their abilities to learn new tricks.

*Above: Boise on the terrace, waiting
to rehearse*
*Below: The railing where the cats
performed their tricks*

> *Uncle Wolfer is in beautiful fur, and is so anxious
> to be popular. He never makes messes anymore and
> will run on a cat race and now have trained him
> and Boise to make a pyramid like lions at the circus
> on the pillars on the front porch. They walk toward
> each other along the railing when called. Uncle
> Wolfer wants to practice it all day long.*

Uncle Wolfer (aka Wolfer, Uncle Wolfie, Stoopy
Wolfer) was one of the many sons of Princessa and
Boise. A warm, friendly cat, he had inherited the
delicate sensibilities of his Persian mother. Conservative
in nature, Wolfer seldom tried anything new, including
Hemingway's home-grown catnip. Ernest wrote about
the cat's finicky tastes in *Islands in the Stream:*

> *Uncle Wolfie would never try anything new and would sniff cautiously at any food
> until the other cats had taken it all and he was left with nothing.*

Long-haired and smoke gray like his mother, Princessa, Uncle Wolfer stood out from
the rest of the cat family. Because of his silver gray coat that turned lighter as he matured,
Ernest referred to him as the Snow Leopard. Like Boise and Good Will, Uncle Wolfer
adored Hemingway and was willing to do anything to please his master. Although
considered debonair and quite timid, like his father, Boise, Uncle Wolfer adapted well to
being trained by Ernest to do tricks.

Michael Pollard, author of *The Encyclopedia of the Cat,* wrote: "Cats always preserve their
own dignity and reserve and, unlike dogs, are not particularly eager to please their owners.

They can rarely be taught to do tricks, not because they are less intelligent than dogs but because they simply do not see the point. If they want to master a particular skill . . . they will do so because the reward is immediate and personal." There is no doubt Hemingway had a special relationship with his cats and they adored their master.

As a child Ernest loved the circus and was fascinated with the big cats, the bears, and the elephants. This interest would continue into adulthood, and he'd catch the animal acts whenever the circus was in town. Hemingway's sister Marcelline Hemingway Sanford recalled in *At the Hemingways:* "From our youngest days on, Daddy took us to the Ringling Brothers Circus at the Coliseum in Chicago every spring. Ernest and I saw our first circus in May, 1902, when I was four and Ernest not yet three. I vaguely remember that first thrilling experience. I was so excited by the noise, the animal smells, the popcorn and peanuts. . . . Ernest always hung back to watch the leopards and the lions pacing in their cages."

Above: Hemingway playing soldier with a boyhood friend, and sister Ursula
Below: Ernest wearing his favorite safari outfit

Hemingway's close friend, A.E. Hotchner, remembered how Hemingway loved the circus animals and wrote about this memory in his biography, *Papa Hemingway:* "One of the few things about New York that Ernest unreservedly enjoyed was the visits of the Ringling Brothers Circus. He felt that circus animals were not like other animals, that they were more intelligent and, because of their constant working alliance with man, had much more highly developed personalities. The first time I went to the circus with him, he was so eager to see the animals he went to Madison Square Garden an hour before the doors were to open. We went around to a side entrance of Fiftieth Street and Ernest banged on the door until an attendant appeared. He tried to turn us away but Ernest had a card signed by his old friend John Ringling North, which stated that the bearer was to be admitted to the circus any time, any place."

It was not only circuses that attracted the young Hemingway. He was also fascinated with battles and hunting wild game. Grace Hall wrote of her son: "Ernest Miller at 51/2 years old is a little man. . . . [He]collects cartoons of the Russo-Japanese War." Ernest's son Gregory, in his autobiography, *Papa: A Personal Memoir,* said that Hemingway read the Bible cover to cover because there were so many battle scenes to read about.

Hemingway's father taught his six children to shoot at an early age. Madelaine Hemingway Miller recalled in her biography *Ernie Hemingway's Sister "Sunny" Remembers:* "We used the grassy hill next to us [at Walloon Lake] for clay-pigeon shooting. The small children graduated from pulling the trap to being allowed to shoot if they wished. . . . Dad taught Ernie to be an excellent shot and was proud of him. Each of us children was taught to handle guns. I preferred the 20 gauge to the .12."

Ernest's grandfather Anson Hemingway gave him his first gun at age ten, a twenty-gauge, single-barrel shotgun. Ernest's father, a superb marksman and hunter, taught his son how to care for his gun, how to hunt down, kill, and dress a deer, and even how to make his own bullets. According to Ernest's grandson Sean Hemingway in *Hemingway on Hunting*. ". . . for any young boy growing up in the first two decades of the twentieth century, it was Theodore Roosevelt . . . western rancher and huntsmen, President of the United States, and later African hunter and South American explorer . . . who inspired the imagination and fueled the desire to explore and hunt in the great outdoors. Hemingway identified with much of Teddy Roosevelt's prowess, enthusiasm and determination. In 1910 when Roosevelt came to Oak Park on a whistle-stop tour after his African safari of the previous year, Ernest in his own little khaki safari outfit, was standing alongside his grandfather Anson, cheering on the great African hunter and rough rider of San Juan Hill. More than any other individual in his time, Roosevelt opened the African frontier to the imagination of America's youths. The fresh scent of a new frontier and the thrill of the hunt, both with their overwhelming sense of valor and excitement, would captivate Hemingway for the rest of his life."

In his lifetime, Hemingway would hunt lions in Africa, mostly marauding lions who had killed villagers and livestock, but he had been so impressed by the elephants he saw in the circuses as a child that, while on safari in Africa, he refused to shoot an elephant, saying that elephants were too magnificent to kill. Ernest knew elephants were devoted parents and were also known to mourn their dead. Hemingway wrote in his novel *The Garden of Eden* about the brutal killing of an old rogue elephant, an animal he held in high esteem. Ernest may have remembered back to the African safari in 1933 when friend Charles Thompson killed his first elephant, or when on a hunting trip as a boy with his father he was expected to make his first kill of a deer and the remorse he may have felt.

David had stood still and listened to the elephant feeding. He could smell him as strongly as he had the night in the moonlight when he had worked up close to him and had seen his wonderful tusks. . . . Then there had been a . . . shot . . . by his father's .450, . . . and he [the elephant] had gone into the heavy growth. . . . They found him anchored, in such suffering and despair that he could no longer move. . . . David saw the blood coming from his flanks and running down his sides. . . . he was down with his shoulder broken. He did not move but his eye was alive and looked at David. . . . He had very long eyelashes and his eye was the most alive thing David had ever seen. "Shoot him" . . . his father said. "Go on." "You shoot him," David had said. . . . The eye of the elephant had opened wide on the first shot and then started to glaze and blood came out of the ear and ran into bright streams down the wrinkled gray hide. . . . Now all the dignity and majesty and all the beauty was gone from the elephant. . . . His father had known how he had felt about the elephant and that night and in the next few days he had tried if not to convert him to bring him back to the boy he had been before he had come to the knowledge that he hated elephant hunting. . . . The elephant was his hero now as his father had been for a long time. . . . The tusks were stained with the dried blood and he scraped some of it off with his thumbnail like a dried piece of sealing wax and put it in the pocket of his shirt. That was all he took from the elephant except the beginning of the knowledge of loneliness.

Hemingway missed his cats, especially Friendless and Boise, when he was at sea aboard the Pilar.

chapter 15

No Cats on the *Pilar*

Probably would have been a hell
of a boat cat . . . except for the spraying.

Islands in the Stream

Hemingway was concerned about the war raging in Europe. Carlos Baker in his biography, *Ernest Hemingway: A Life Story,* wrote: "Other writers might lend talents to propagandizing as John Steinbeck had done for the Air Force with *Bombs Away* but Ernest said emphatically that he would rather cut three fingers off his throwing hand than write such a book. He was willing to go to the war himself, or send his sons as they came of age, or contribute such money as he could command. But he was unwilling to write anything official unless it could be " 'absolute truth' . . . a manifest impossibility in war times." But Hemingway was also concerned about what was happening at home in Cuba. Ernest had been involved with a private intelligence network during the Spanish Civil War in 1937 and felt a similar operation should be organized in Cuba. While working on his *Men at War* anthology for Crown

Above: Hemingway would be at sea for weeks at a time looking for Nazi subs. Hemingway named his sub-chasing mission after his favorite stud cat, Friendless, below.

Publishing in New York his desire to go to war became even stronger, but at the time he was more worried about incidents happening at home rather than abroad.

German submarines were wreaking havoc in the Caribbean. Hemingway estimated an average of one hundred allied boats a month were being sunk and hundreds of lives lost. All this was happening in the same waters where he had fished for years for marlin, tuna, and shark.

He also knew that the hard-working Cuban fishermen he so admired and had come to call his friends were at risk. Hemingway's plan was to equip his thirty-eight-foot yacht, the *Pilar,* as a Q-boat with enough artillery to sink or disable a Nazi submarine. The code name for the eight men who formed his crew was "The Crook Factory." The code name for the dangerous operation was "Friendless," named after Hemingway's big, tough, but loveable, black stud cat, a cat he would have liked to have taken onboard the *Pilar* except for his notorious spraying. Hemingway reminisced about his big black cat in *Islands in the Stream:*

> At sea he used to think about Goats [Friendless] as well as Boise. But there
> was nothing tragic about Goats. Although he had been through some truly bad
> times he was absolutely entire and, even when he had been beaten in some of
> his most terrible fights, he was never pitiful. Even when he had not been able
> to walk up to the house and lay under the mango tree below the terrace panting
> and soaked wet with sweat so you saw how big his shoulders were and how
> narrow and thin his flanks, lying there, too dead to move, trying to get the air
> into his lungs, he was never pitiful. He had the wide head of a lion and he was
> as unbeaten. Goats was fond of the man, and Thomas Hudson was fond of him
> and respected and loved him.

Hemingway also considered bringing Boise aboard the boat. He desperately missed his cat friend when he was at sea, but Boise preferred not to travel. According to son Patrick in *Hemingway on War,* "Ernest was the healthiest and happiest at sea." Having his cats aboard would have added to his contentment.

Martha did not take her husband's plans to chase down enemy submarines seriously. She felt it was their duty as war correspondents to get as close to the front lines in Europe as possible and report on the war. Ernest had spent much of the past ten years of his life fishing the same waters which were now being invaded by the Germans. He felt his duty was at home defending his country as well as the island nation he now called home.

After five years associated with Hemingway, Martha Gellhorn's patience was growing thin and their marriage was starting to unravel. Carlos Baker quoted Ellis Briggs, Ernest's friend from the American Embassy in Cuba, in *Ernest Hemingway: A Life Story:* "His hours were unpredictable; his associates were innumerable, noisy, and often unwashed; his personal untidiness was more than matched by a 'ghastly collection of in-bred cats' which roamed the Finca's interiors at will and left their filth in odd corners. It was fun to be a guest there, . . . and Ernest could be the kindest and most considerate of hosts, but it must have been undiluted hell to try to have any organized life with him." During the months of submarine chasing it had definitely become a man's world at the Finca.

The only stabilizing force for Martha Gellhorn during this

Hemingway looks for German submarines aboard the Pilar.

trying time of her life was the writing of her novel, *Liana,* with her favorite cat, Thruster, constantly by her side. Martha had decided that when she finished her book she would accept an assignment with *Colliers* to report on the war from England. With her husband almost continuously at sea Martha felt she was not needed at home and could serve her country best by going abroad. Martha's Jewish heritage may have also had a lot to do with her strong desire to see and report on the war firsthand.

One of the cats that Martha Gellhorn had sterilized by the town veterinarian.

To care for their house, grounds, and ever-expanding family of cats and dogs, Martha and Ernest had hired enough servants, including a Chinese cook whose pet parrot could imitate a cat fight. But Martha continued to worry about the cats that were inbreeding at an alarming rate and felt that something needed to be done. Ernest was focused on locating enemy subs and said that the cat problems would have to wait.

When Martha's favorite cat Thruster (aka Thrusty) went into her first heat, to Martha's dismay, the young female mated with her father Boise, producing two blind kittens. Hemingway named both kittens Blindie. He may have felt their chances of surviving were slim and that it was likely that only one would survive to claim the name. Despite the kittens' afflictions, both did survive, with the stronger of the two growing into adulthood.

Martha felt the inbreeding of the Finca cats was the direct cause of the kittens' blindness and decided to take the matter into her own hands. While Hemingway was out on one of his many submarine scouting trips aboard the *Pilar,* Gellhorn had all the adult cats sterilized by the town's vet. One of the cats died because of complications from the surgery. When Ernest returned home and found out what his wife had done to the cats, he went into a violent rage. Martha had destroyed all his hopes of starting a new breed of cat with his purebred Persian Princessa, his adopted Cuban stray cat Boise, and the Angora tiger cat Good Will. Hemingway never forgave his wife for her actions, telling friends that "she cut my cats." The younger male cats Friendless and Fatso were saved from the knife because of their young age. These cats became Hemingway's pride and joy and soon became the principal stud cats of the family.

Martha's actions may have inadvertently prolonged the lives of the older male cats at the Finca. The surgeries made the adult male cats less aggressive and less likely to challenge Friendless and Fatso as the young males grew older. In fact, Boise became so loving and laid back that he preferred being an inside cat except when climbing mango trees in search of fruit rats, thus leaving the up-and-coming stud cats to do the battling for power and for mates.

Martha left Cuba for Europe on October 25, 1943. She would miss her day and night companion, Thruster, whom she had raised from a kitten. Martha hoped to be in London by early November.

Hemingway planned a three-month cruise aboard the *Pilar,* but the weather did not cooperate. It was one of the coldest winters he could remember in the Caribbean, and he missed Martha, who was now somewhere in Europe. According to Carlos Baker in *Ernest Hemingway: A Life Story,* Hemingway complained to his son Patrick in a letter:

"... the icy surf was breaking over the bar all across the harbor entrance. The cats at the Finca were probably cold, too, and if the hard weather held he would go home to see them. He missed the cats and his younger kids. It was no use to miss Marty and Bumby because they were too far away."

Hemingway would later write his ex-wife Hadley on November 25. Martha had been gone one month and he was terribly lonely. He told Hadley he had only his cats and dogs for company.

... there are eleven cats here. One cat just leads to another. The mother is Tester a Persian from the Silver Dawn Cattery somewhere in Florida. She had a kitten named Thruster out of Dillinger a black and white cat from Cojimar a coastal fishing village. By the same sire she also bore Furhouse, Fats, Friendless and Friendless's Brother. All in the same litter. Two lovely black Persian appearings and two Black and Whites like Dingie. We also have a grey, sort of snow leopard cat named Uncle Wolfer (Persian) and a Tiger cat from Guanabacoa named Good Will after Nelson Rockefeller. There are at present two half grown kittens named Blindie (on acct. of Blindness. Born that way) daughters of Thruster and her own father. That shows us the fat lady? And Nuisance Value also known as Littless Kitty who is the most beautiful of all. ...

The front terrace was a popular gathering place for the Finca cats.

The place is so damned big it doesn't really seem as though there were many cats until you see them all moving like a mass migration at feeding time. We also have 5 dogs, one good pointer [Lem] and the others small mongrels on the style of Wax Puppy. It is wonderful when Marty and/or the kids are here but it is lonesome as a bastard when I'm here alone. I have taught Uncle Wolfer, Dillinger and Will to walk along the railings to the porch pillars and make a pyramid like lions and have taught Friendless to drink with me (Whiskey and milk) but even that doesn't take the place of a wife and family.

Hemingway missed his wife and his three sons, and he still had hopes that he would eventually have more children, especially a daughter—if not with Martha, possibly with someone else. Gellhorn returned to the Finca in March of 1944. She hoped to convince her husband to return with her to

Europe. But according to Carlos Baker in *Ernest Hemingway: A Life Story:* ". . . he did not seem to be in any great hurry to depart. On the last day of January, he wrote his wife that he still had no special interest in Europe. He merely felt like an old horse being saddled for the jumps by an unscrupulous owner."

Hemingway did take the war seriously, but felt he was needed on the homefront. As he wrote in *For Whom the Bell Tolls*, the loss of life in the Caribbean from German submarine attacks was serious enough.

> *When we have just seen the sky full of airplanes of a quality to kill us back to our grandfathers and forward to all unborn grandsons including all cats, goats and bedbugs. Airplanes making a noise to curdle the milk in your mother's breasts as they pass over darkening the sky and roaring like lions and you ask me to take things seriously. I take them too seriously already.*

On May 13, 1944, Martha found passage from New York on a cargo ship loaded with dynamite. She would dock in Liverpool on May 27. Despite his initial reservations, Ernest accepted an assignment from *Collier's* magazine. He would serve as their frontline war correspondent. Ernest arranged for a flight to London from New York that would depart on May 17.

While in New York waiting for his flight orders, Hemingway visited with friend and novelist Dawn Powell. Powell, also a cat fancier, remembered a humorous moment when her cat looked out from behind a curtain at the large, burly visitor. Powell told Hemingway her cat reminded her of a house detective and began to laugh. According to Carlos Baker in *Ernest Hemingway A Life Story*, Powell said that Ernest told her, "Never laugh at a cat. . . . Dogs like it because they want to be pals with you. Cats don't want to be pals; they must be kings and queens." Hemingway complained to Powell that he was still mad at Martha because she had left their home in Cuba without saying goodbye to her favorite cat Thruster. Thruster would miss her mistress, and unfortunately the next mistress of the Finca Vigia would not be as kind.

It was Hemingway's first visit to London, and his reunion with his wife did not go well. Her long absences from home and her desire to postpone motherhood had taken its toll on the relationship.

Mary Welsh, a petite blonde who was working at the London Bureau of *Time, Life*, and *Fortune*, was also having misgivings about marriage to her husband, Australian journalist Noel Monks. In her diary January 1, 1944, she wrote "no children . . . and feeling at times a stranger to Noel."

Mary had already heard that the American writer Ernest Hemingway was in town and she wanted to meet him. She had recently met and had a brief affair with Ernest's younger brother, Leicester, who was in London as part of a documentary film crew, and she now focused her attention on Ernest. Mary had no reservations about taking advantage of lonely servicemen away from home, whether married or not. Like her husband, Noel, Hemingway was a big man, but he was also a celebrity writer who commanded attention wherever he went. Mary liked that. She liked being noticed, and Ernest Hemingway brought notice to whomever he was with.

Mary managed to meet Hemingway shortly after he arrived in London. According to Welsh in her autobiography *How It Was*, "I sensed an air of solitude about him, loneliness perhaps, and dismissed it. He was a newcomer with few friends. We found a day when both of us were free for lunch." A few evenings later Hemingway stopped by Mary's room at the Dorchester Hotel. She and friend Connie Ernst had conveniently decided to rent a hotel room in the same hotel where Ernest was staying. Whatever Mary did to attract Ernest's attention worked. Hemingway was falling in love with the petite blonde journalist he fondly called Kitten or Kittner.

One person who did not approve of the new woman in Hemingway's life was singer, film star, and good friend Marlene Dietrich, who was introduced to Mary by Ernest in

Ernest Hemingway and good friend Marlene Dietrich

1944 at the Ritz in Paris. According to biographer Steven Bach in *Marlene Dietrich: Life and Legend,* Dietrich found Mary to be "stiff, formal and not very desirable." Hemingway had first met Dietrich in 1934 during an Atlantic crossing aboard the *Ile de France.* They never became lovers—Hemingway had said the timing was never right—but his admiration for the beautiful blonde German whom he fondly called "the Kraut" could not be concealed. Dietrich referred to Hemingway as "the pope of my church." Hemingway also admired Marlene's courage. She had not only put herself in harm's way to entertain the troops in Europe during World War II, but was said to have offered her services to the Office of Strategic Services (forerunner of the Central Intelligence Agency). Hemingway and Dietrich's friendship would span more than a quarter of a century.

According to Christopher Ondaatje in *Hemingway in Africa: The Last Safari,* "Hemingway was a man who needed to be married. He also needed romance. It drove him and was also the engine of all his stories. In providing material for his writing, his romances were every bit as important as his he-man adventures."

But in the spring of 1944 the war called, and Hemingway left London for the frontlines on the continent. According to Ernest's grandson Sean Hemingway in *Hemingway On War,* Ernest in his lifetime witnessed and recorded most of the major wars of the first half of the twentieth century. During his ten months in Europe during World War II, Hemingway would fly reconnaissance missions with the Royal Air Force, experience the devastating bombings of London by the Germans, and be on hand for the D-Day landing at Normandy and the liberation of his beloved Paris. Also under combat conditions he would report on the Allied infantry's heroic movement into Germany. Colonel (later General) C.T. (Buck) Landon, the Regimental Commander of the First Army's Fourth Infantry Division who became a close friend and confidant of Hemingway during the war, referred to Ernest in Denis Brian's book *The True Gen: An*

Intimate Portrait of Hemingway by Those Who Knew Him as "battle wise, smart as hell on the battlefield" and under fire the bravest man that Landon had ever known.

When Ernest Hemingway returned home to Cuba the first week of April, 1945, he found his Cuban estate had been devastated by the October 1944 hurricane. In an undated letter to his wife Martha Gellhorn (they were now officially separated) he wrote:

> *Hurricane in its effect on grounds too sad to talk about. But most of the best royals remain and place still more beautiful than any other I've ever seen. Big Ceiba [tree] and most flamboyan-tes fine. Anyone who hasn't seen it before would think it was the way it had been planned I guess We lost all the best mango trees; most of the key royal palms looking off toward the Mts. No use listing all the losses. Were plenty. But place and grounds essentially intact.*

What really troubled Hemingway was the deplorable condition of his cat family. A cat, one of the two Blindies, blind since birth but who against all odds had grown into a healthy and thriving member of the clan, had died in the storm. In the letter he wrote:

> *When I got home the cotsies looked like something out of Daschau. It was heart-breaking. Have them all o.k. now. Blindie drowned in the hurricane. All other cats o.k.*

The ancient ceiba tree on the Finca's front terrace survived the storm.

Friendless' Brother and Willy, two of Hemingway's favorite cats, kept him company while he wrote.

Mary Welsh was now the new woman in Hemingway's life but, as before, he found himself in love with two women. This time it was Mary who had captured his heart, although he was still in love with Martha. But Martha was seldom home and Hemingway was desperately lonely at the time. Still he was guilt-ridden by the fact he was leaving his third wife for another woman.

In a letter he wrote Martha:

> *Dearest Mook if you want to marry anyone or have any urgency for the divorce will go downtown tomorrow and start it no matter what repercussions on me or others. You have a right to anything you want. But if there is no hurry*

and the separation status is adequate will get it the soonest it is tactically most favourable considering the angles that exist and have come up. If it is a question of telling people you might tell them we are divorcing in a month or a couple of months or in the fall. Please know I will never stall on it. If can swing right away you can just tell them we are divorcing sooner than we expected.

Don't know how is with you but terrible hard for me to write immediately after war. As though all the taste buds were burned off and as though you had heard so much loud music you couldn't hear anything played delicately. But I promise you I will try to get in as good as shape as I can be and write as well as I can to make up (there is no such thing) for all the things we lost.

Hemingway ended the letter to Martha with an invitation to use the Cuban house whenever she wanted.

Will be nice to see Childries. Wish you were seeing them too. But see no reason why if you ever have a place we can't split them with you if you want them. Also if you and Mother ever want to use this place no reason why not. . . .

Ernest would always consider Gellhorn the first mistress of Finca Vigia. Martha had been the one who had actually found the estate and encouraged Ernest to rent it. She was also almost as fond of the Finca cats as Hemingway, a man she once fondly referred to as Big Kitten. Years later, Martha Gellhorn would tell Valerie Hemingway that, as lovers, she and Ernest were fine, but marriage had been a disaster.

When the two first met, Hemingway was instantly attracted to journalist Mary Welsh.

chapter 16

A Wildcat in Bed

*. . . he had seen Princessa in heat, not the first tragic
time, but after she was grown and beautiful, and so
suddenly changed from all her dignity and poise
into wantonness. . . .*

Islands in the Stream

Ernest Hemingway found it hard to look his younger brother, Leicester, in the face
when he saw him at a London hospital in 1944. Ernest had been hospitalized with
lacerations and a severe concussion from a car accident. He said Leicester looked too
much like their mother, a woman Ernest now said he hated and blamed for the suicide
death of their father. However, it may not have been Leicester's resemblance to his
mother, Grace—tall, blonde, and blue-eyed—that upset Ernest. It may have been the fact
that Ernest knew his younger brother had had an affair with Mary Welsh before he had
entered the picture.

Leicester may have been introduced to Mary by writer and film documentarian Irwin
Shaw at the White Tower Restaurant in SoHo, a place frequented by the foreign press and
the military. Irwin Shaw had also been one of Mary's lovers during the war and belonged
to the same documentary film unit as Ernest's brother. Leicester was a tall, strikingly
handsome young man, and it was easy to see why Mary might have been attracted to
him. Although married, he had told Ernest the relationship with his wife, Patricia Shedd,
like so many long-distance romances, wasn't working out. Mary may have worried that
Ernest might learn of her affair with his younger brother and decided to tell him. "Les,
out of respect for his older brother, never told Ernest about his affair with Mary," said
Leicester's second wife, Doris Hemingway. Ernest's relationship with his brother cooled
considerably after Hemingway and Welsh were married.

Hemingway wrote good friend Sara Murphy on May 5, 1945, explaining why he
and Martha had broken up and about the new woman in his life. Sara had been one of
Hemingway's closest confidants for many years.

> *Marty and I split up its hard to say exactly where. But I need a wife in bed
> and not just in even the most widely circulated magazines. Been in love with a
> girl named Mary Welsh since last June. She wants to quit work and have children
> and look after me and I need that plenty. Also she is great believer in bed which I
> believe is probably my true Patria and we carved as good a life as anybody could
> make under the circumstances right out of the middle of the worst times you can
> imagine.*

Martha divorced Ernest on December 21, 1946, but she remained a woman he still
admired, respected, and loved. Although Hemingway would continue to call Mary Welsh
nicknames he had used while courting her in Europe, such as Kitten and Kittner, it was
obvious Mary was to Hemingway more like a wildcat in bed.

Boise was fond of Hemingway's new blonde female friend.

chapter 17

Mary Welsh and the Cats' Tower

Dogs is trumps but cats is the
longest suit we hold.

How It Was

It was important to Ernest Hemingway
in 1945 that his bride-to-be, Mary Welsh,
like the sea and his family of cats and
dogs. Ernest lucked out on all accounts.
Mary loved the sea, was comfortable
aboard the *Pilar,* and became an excellent
angler. Mary also was enchanted by the
family of small dogs with the curled
tails, particularly Negrita, a female dog
Hemingway had rescued from the
streets of Havana, and she had a genuine
fondness for his beloved feline friends.
She immediately took to the Finca's
principal cat family that consisted of
Princessa, Boise, Friendless, Friendless's

*Ernest and Mary display new litters of the Finca kittens
and puppies.*

Brother, Willy, Uncle Wolfer, Good Will, Fatso, Furhouse, Thruster, and Littless Kitty. It wasn't
long after Mary's arrival that Thruster, Martha's favorite cat, gave birth to three energetic males.
Ernest decided to name two of the brothers after poets. He felt cats liked to hear the sound of
"s" in their names and christened one Stephen Spender, which was changed to Spendthrift and
shortened to Spendy. Spendy's brother was named Shakespeare, changed to Barbershop and later
again changed to Shopsky. The third kitten of the triplets was named Ecstasy. Ernest and Mary
took great patience to teach each cat his name on the front terrace of the Finca under garlands of
bright red bougainvillea, rewarding them with treats of catnip. Spendy immediately bonded with
Hemingway's new female friend and became Mary's "love sponge" and constant companion.
Boise was also enchanted with the new mistress of Finca Vigia, and soon developed a crush on the
petite blonde with the sweet scent of *My Sin* perfume, bringing Mary gifts of half-dead fruit rats
and depositing them on her bedroom window ledge. Hemingway described one of these times in
Islands in the Stream:

> Boise was a very silent cat. But he called to the man as soon as he was on
> the window ledge and Thomas Hudson went to the screen and opened it. Boise
> leaped in. He had two fruit rats in his mouth. In the moonlight that came in
> through the window, throwing the shadow of the trunk of the cieba tree across
> the wide, white bed, Boise had played with the fruit rats. Leaping and turning,

Mary found the Finca cats well behaved, but felt they needed their own room.

batting them along the floor, and then carrying one away to crouch and rush the other, he had played as wildly as when he was a kitten. Then he carried them into the bathroom and after that Thomas Hudson had felt his weight as he jumped on the bed. "So you weren't eating mangoes out of trees?" the man had asked him. Boise rubbed his head against him. "So you were hunting and looking after the property? My old cat and brother Boise. Aren't you going to eat them now you have them?" Boise had only rubbed his head against the man and purred with his silent purr and then, because he was tired from the hunt, he had gone to sleep. But he had slept restlessly and in the morning he had shown no interest in the dead fruit rats at all.

When Mary Welsh arrived at the Finca, Thruster (aka Thrusty) tried to make friends with the new visitor, desperately lonesome for female companionship after her mistress, Martha Gellhorn, had left the Finca for the last time. But Mary, after being told by

Ernest that Thruster had been Martha's favorite cat, wanted no part of the lonely feline. Mary wrote in *How It Was* that Thruster was clawing her sheet, asking for affection and she had written in her diary: "Thrusty mistakes me, I am not hers, nor she mine."

The cat family had the run of the house, sleeping in the guest bedroom on two double beds. The room was situated in the center of the home, off the spacious living room, with a door opening to the back terrace, where the cats were fed. The Finca's houseboy, Rene Villarreal, lovingly cared for the cats and served the ever-growing menagerie bowls of ground meat, canned salmon, turtle meat when available, and fresh milk from the farm's cows, as well as treats of homegrown catnip when available. Boise preferred people food to the cat food, dining on whatever Ernest ate.

Boise would climb into Mary's bedroom through the open windows to bring her gifts of fruit rats.

Ernest's breakfast was usually served in his bedroom while he worked. Rene would also include several bowls of food for the cats in attendance. The cats were Ernest's constant companions and Hemingway said they helped him in his work. Boise received preferential treatment, sitting by Ernest's side while he wrote.

Mary Welsh was enchanted by Finca Vigia on her arrival on May 2, 1945. But by August she was having second thoughts about the large cat family that had taken up residence in the guest bedroom of the house.

Above: The guest room no longer accommodated the growing cat family. Below: Mary with her companion, Negrita

Even though Mary was fond of Hemingway's feline friends, she felt the cats needed to have their own room, possibly separate from the main house—particularly Ernest's stud cats that had a terrible habit of spraying. During a visit to Hemingway's home in Cuba, Ernest's sister, Madelaine Hemingway Miller, wrote in *Ernest Hemingway's Sister "Sunny" Remembers:* "The bedroom between the living room and the veranda was the cat room. A couple of single beds and cushions were strewn about, as well as eating and drinking dishes to accommodate the scores of cats that kept accumulating. The room had a door that would swing in and out so the cats could come in and go at their pleasure, day or night. Cases of salmon were fed to them."

Boise, one of Hemingway's dearest cat friends

Hemingway and Boise enjoyed daily walks together.

Mary thought the guest bedroom could better serve Hemingway if it was made into additional library space for his expanding book collection. The guest bedroom could still be used for guests, if needed, but the two-story guest house (known as the *Casita*) next door was big enough to accommodate family and friends.

Hemingway had read in *Care and Handling of CATS: A Manual For Modern Cat Owners* by Doris Bryant, published in 1944, a book he kept on the table next to his side of the bed in Mary's bedroom, that "A mature male should have his own quarters—a large and sunny room where he can spray and howl and be entirely natural and normal. In a bare room, it is easy to wipe up after a cat that has sprayed. . . . And no male should be scolded or punished for spraying or howling, it would just be as reasonable to punish him for eating or sleeping." Mary's idea of a separate house for the cats began to make sense to Hemingway, and he agreed that they needed more space for the cats. He told Mary that he would build a house for the cats close to their house, but he was worried that the cats might feel rejected and hurt if they were moved too far from the main building. Mary was visiting family and friends in late September when Ernest wrote her about his thoughts on a new home for the cats.

Above: When the cats were moved to their room in the tower, the guestroom gained added library space.
Below: Hemingway often turned to his favorite cat care book for help.

> *Want to get good small house for the cotsies now . . . with easily cleaned arrangements and nice shelves to sleep on and places to have and raise their kittens. . . . It ought to be almost part of house so cotsies do not feel sent to Siberia or abandoned and it should be close enough so that from house you can see whether it is well cared for and cotsies will be happy. . . . Will make a big scratching pole covered with carpet for them to use their claws on and have catnip bin and*

Friendless' Brother kept Hemingway company while he worked.

Hemingway did not want his cats to feel abandoned if they moved to new quarters next to the main house. Two cats bask in the morning sun as Princessa, right, looks on.

> *ping-pong balls for kittneys to play with. Can even put in Shakespeare First Folio for Friendless to spray on* [an act which Friendless had already committed]. *It is unfair to keep cotsies, not feed them properly, and interpret their natural impulses and needs as sins.*

Hemingway enjoyed the closeness of his cats underfoot, but Mary was pleased with the plans for a new cat house for their expanding cat family, allowing the principal cats to remain in the house if they wished, particularly Boise, who was Ernest's day and night companion.

Ernest and Mary were married March 14, 1946, but it would be almost a year before plans were drawn up and construction began on the structure. Edwardo Rivero, the principal building contractor from the village of San Francisco de Paula, was hired to do the work. Ernest and Mary decided on a four-story building which Hemingway referred

The Finca cats patiently wait on the back terrace for their meals.

to as "the tower." The building would be four meters eighty centimeters square and twelve meters (forty feet) high above the ground level, with a patio on the roof where Mary could sunbathe nude. The staircase would run outside the building, offering a spectacular view of the countryside.

The four-story tower under construction

The cats' room would be on the second floor of the tower on the level with the terrace. It was important to Hemingway that he would be able to see the cats' room from a window in his bedroom and also from a window in his bathroom, where he stood every morning while he shaved. The cats' room would also be in close proximity to the doors of the dining room, kitchen, and the back terrace, where the cats were fed. Hemingway envisioned the cats' new room as having large windows, providing good light and cross ventilation. He wanted tile on the floor, making the room easier to wash down and clean. The first ground-floor room, below the cats' room, would house a much-needed carpentry shop for their Spanish carpenter Pancho. The third-floor room would serve for extra storage for Hemingway's fishing and hunting gear, their winter clothes, and their luggage, and could be used as an additional guest bedroom. A workroom on the fourth floor would offer Hemingway the privacy in which to write.

Times had changed a lot for Hemingway since his poverty years in Paris when he said he was too poor to own a cat. Not only was he a successful writer, but he could afford to take care of as many cats as he could possibly desire. By 1954 he and Mary would own thirty-four cats and the colony would continue to grow. Hemingway would surprise friends by identifying and naming each and every cat.

The cats' room on the second floor was light, airy, and easy to clean.

When Earl Wilson of the *New York Post* said that there were those asking if Ernest was a true American citizen since he preferred to live in Cuba instead of the United States, Ernest fired back:

> *You find me a place in Ohio where I can live on top of a hill and be fifteen minutes away from the Gulf Stream and have my own fruits and vegetables the year around and raise and fight fame chickens without breaking the law and I'll go live in Ohio if Miss Mary and my cats and dogs agree.*

Hemingway loved Cuba and its people and could not imagine living or working anywhere else. A revolutionary war would change all that.

Boise could always sense when Hemingway was leaving on a trip.

chapter 18

Miss Kitty of the Wild West

*. . . an unfortunate cat who
had many sorrows and occasional ecstasies. . .*
Islands in the Stream

In July 1946 Mary learned she was pregnant. Ernest was delighted, and he and Mary planned a vacation out West to celebrate the event. Hemingway wrote well in the cool mountain air of Sun Valley, Idaho. He also felt the climate would be good for his wife, hoping she would provide him the daughter he had always wanted.

Hemingway had begun writing a new novel, *The Garden of Eden,* in the early months of his marriage to Mary. One of the storylines of his new fiction strongly resembled his marriage, and the character, Catherine Bourne, resembled his wife, the once sexually promiscuous blonde, whom he fondly called "devil." This was also a nickname Hemingway used for Catherine in his novel.

Hemingway was pleased when he learned Mary was pregnant.

Ernest's and Mary's hopes of having a daughter were ended on the night of August 18 in Casper, Wyoming, when Mary awoke in extreme pain. Mary was taken by ambulance to the county hospital. Unfortunately, the chief surgeon was on a fishing trip, a three- or four-hour drive from Casper. Ernest was informed by the doctor on duty that Mary was hemorrhaging from a ruptured fallopian tube. According to Mary, in her autobiography *How It Was,* "it did not occur to me that the happenings inside of me could be fatal, which is perhaps why my heart continued beating after my veins had collapsed and there was nothing but a trickle of blood for it to pump. . . . I heard Ernest's voice beside me on the operating table and saw his rubber-gloved hands milking plasma down into my left arm." Biographer Michael Reynolds wrote in *Hemingway: The Final Years:* "The doctor told Ernest it was hopeless, if he operated, Mary would die from shock. It was time to tell her goodbye. Ernest, who had seen enough battlefield transfusions . . . took charge. Quite literally, Ernest's quick and effective decisions brought Mary back from the edge of death." Mary was released from the hospital September 3, but it would be another week before the woman Hemingway fondly called "Kitten" would be able to travel.

A friend, Lloyd "Pappy" Arnold, chief photographer of the Union Pacific at Sun Valley, found Ernest and Mary a rental cabin in Ketchum, Idaho, a charming small village that had once been a prosperous mining town, just one mile from the Sun Valley ski resort. The cabin was actually a series of rooms, an addition built onto the office of the MacDonald Cabins, but spacious enough to house Ernest, Mary, and Hemingway's three sons, who were visiting. Mary recovered quickly in the beautiful surroundings.

It was a marvelous season of hunting trips and social functions with good friends and family. The weather cooperated fully, and Ernest's work was going well. Mary described one of the lovely days in *How It Was:* "Glorious afternoon . . . making forays into acres of sagebrush surrounding the fields, breathing the pungent air of autumn-earth and grasses. . . ."

While returning from a duck hunt, Mary and Ernest heard the cries of small kittens in the barn behind their cabin. Mary wrote about the incident in *How It Was:* "Somewhere in the recesses of that barn a wild tiger cat had produced a family and one of her daughters joined up with us, adopting Patrick and Papa as bed warmers and me as a climbing trellis and commissary. She was striped, black and gray, with a face like a pansy, convinced that humans in all their parts were made for amusement and the exercise of her athletic skill, and she learned immediately that a change of her voice brought her loving attentions both in food and fondling. Papa named her Miss Kitty, and none of her wild brethren had so good a fall."

Hemingway, although enjoying the delightful change of scenery, missed his Cuban farm and his animals, particularly Boise. Miss Kitty had been a delightful diversion, but on November 10, it was time to say goodbye to their friends. The question was, what to do with Miss Kitty? They certainly could not leave her to "the hazards of a homeless winter," according to Mary. Luckily, they would be visiting their friend Didi Allen in Murray, Utah, for a few days of duck hunting. Didi was also a cat fancier and owned several cats herself, and Miss Kitty quickly joined Didi's menagerie.

Wild cats found shelter in the barns.

Back at home at the Finca, Willy and the triplets, Spendy, Shopsky and Ecstasy, enjoyed a romp in a big tree.

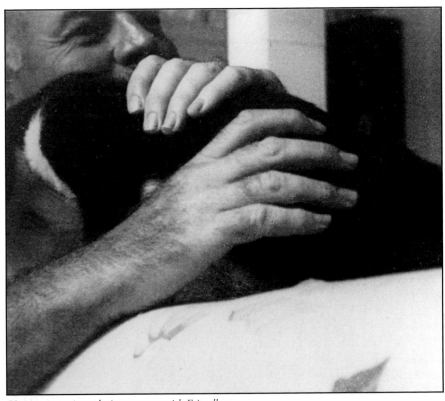

Hemingway enjoys a loving moment with Friendless.

chapter 19

Never Punish a Cat

*Male or female, a cat will show you how
it feels about you. People hide their feelings for
various reasons, but cats never do.*

My Brother, Ernest Hemingway

On June 13, 1947, Ernest Hemingway received a Bronze Star for meritorious service as a war correspondent during his 1944 tour of duty in France and Germany. The citation read as follows: ". . . he displayed a broad familiarity with modern military science, interpreting and evaluating the campaigns and operations of friendly and enemy forces, circulating freely under fire in combat areas in order to obtain an accurate picture of conditions. Through his talent of expression, Mr. Hemingway enabled readers to obtain a vivid picture of the difficulties and triumphs of the front-line soldier and his organization in combat."

The cats Boise and Friendless may have wondered what all the commotion was all about. A steady stream of well-wishers were arriving at the Finca to congratulate

Friendless and his brother, Fatso, relaxing on the terrace

Hemingway on the prestigious honor. Fishing pal and writer S. Kip Farrington Jr. wrote in his book *Fishing with Hemingway and Glassell:* "Cats were welcome at Finca Vigia, but so were people—perhaps too many people. The demands on Ernest's time were enormous, and I often marvel that his literary output was as great as it was." Any personal attention the cats hoped to receive from their master would have to wait another day.

When Hemingway could not find Boise, who often enjoyed hunting for fruit rats in the mango trees of the farm, he would turn to Friendless for company. Friendless (aka Bigotes,

Friendless, one of Hemingway's most beloved cats, was immortalized in his novel Islands in the Stream.

Goats) was the loveable, big black stud cat of the Hemingway household. His mother was the elegant Persian Princessa, and his father was the Cuban cat Boise, from whom he inherited his black and white coloring. Friendless was generally a happy cat who was loved by Ernest, and who Hemingway immortalized in his novel *Islands in the Stream*. Next to Boise, Friendless was one of Hemingway's closest cat friends.

> *On that night he had missed Boise who nearly always walked with him and he had taken Big Goats, one of Boise's sons, a big-shouldered, heavy-necked, wide-faced, tremendous-whiskered, black fighting cat for the walk. Goats never hunted. He was a fighter and a stud cat and that kept him occupied. But he was cheerful, except where his work was concerned and he liked to walk especially if Thomas Hudson would stop every now and then and push him hard with his foot so that he would lie flat on his side. Thomas Hudson would then stroke the cat's belly with his foot. It was difficult to stroke Goats too hard or too roughly, and he would as soon be stroked with a shoe on as barefoot.*

Friendless (aka Bigotes, Goats) was devoted to Hemingway, but had to play second fiddle to his father, Boise, and was always happy when Ernest's attention turned to him.

> *Goats liked him drunk better than sober or, perhaps, it was only when Thomas Hudson was drunk that Goats got to sleep with him that made it seem that way.*
> —Islands in the Stream

No matter if Hemingway was sober or not, Friendless (goats) loved him. Friendless loved to play games with Hemingway, grateful for any attention he received. His favorite game was helping Hemingway look for his medicine. Hemingway would get down on the floor with Friendless and they would both peer under the bed together looking for the missing pills and Friendless would start to purr. Hemingway captured these moments in *Islands in the Stream*:

> *"Goats," [Friendless] he had said, "We have to find the medicine." He had got out of bed and Goats came down on the floor, too, and they hunted for the medicine. Goats went under the bed, not knowing what he was hunting, but doing all he could, and Thomas Hudson said to him, "The medicine, Goats. Find the medicine." Goats made whimpery cries under the bed and ranged all the area. Finally he came out, purring, and Thomas Hudson, feeling over the floor, touched the capsule. It was dusty and cobwebby under his fingers. Goats had found it.*

Hemingway had a problem with Friendless spraying in the house and once remarked to a friend that his stud cat had sprayed the original copy of his letter and he would have to send him the carbon copy. Hemingway did not believe in punishing his cats, agreeing with cat expert and author Doris Bryant in her book *Care and Handling of CATS: A Manual For Modern Cat Owners,* who wrote "scolding or punishing a cat after he has done something does no good, because the cat does not understand. It does however, do harm, because it confuses him and makes him more likely to do irresponsible things. A cat cannot reason and think backward and connect the punishment with what was done. He hasn't the faintest notion what the person is concerned about. He just loses trust in people."

After visiting Ernest and Mary in Cuba, Hemingway's sister Madelaine Hemingway Miller wrote in *Ernest Hemingway's Sister "Sunny" Remembers,* "The cats seem to own the house and we marveled at the patience everyone had with them. It was not at all unusual, time and time again, to have to scatter cats from the breakfast table. The family dog seemed much better behaved."

Hemingway enjoyed the comfort of his cats close by. Friendless' Brother, Fatso and Friendless are underneath the table, keeping Ernest company.

Hemingway with Black Dog on the back terrace of the Finca

chapter 20

Finding Black Dog

*Any small hardships we
encountered seemed to me to
be dwarfed by Blackie's odyssey.*
The Christmas Story
By-Line Ernest Hemingway

In August, 1947, Hemingway's blood
pressure had risen to 215 over 125. He was
also seriously overweight, tipping the scales at
256 pounds, and still suffered from terrible
headaches and sporadic ringing in the ears
from a severe concussion caused by his 1944
car accident. He was also still mourning
the death of his editor, Max Perkins, who
died suddenly on June 17. Of Perkins,
Hemingway had said, "I never had a better
friend." Mary felt a change of scenery might
help, so she suggested a trip to Idaho where
the fresh mountain air seemed to agree with
her husband's fluctuating blood pressure.
Hemingway agreed and purchased a new
Buick Roadmaster convertible for the trip. The
car was a beautiful royal blue with bright red
leather seats. Ernest had arranged with Toby
Bruce, his Key West friend and handyman, to
share in the driving. Mary would fly to Sun
Valley and join her husband at the Sun Valley
Lodge. She described the country in *How It
Was:* "Idaho was providing us with one of its
spectacular, beautiful autumns, its daytime air
shimmering with undiluted sunshine, its nights
cold enough to freeze the water in my bedside
glass." The fresh mountain air did agree with
Hemingway. He lost twenty-eight pounds and
brought his blood pressure down to 150 over

Mary Hemingway with Black Dog

104. Ernest was writing well in the cooler climate of the mountains, writing over eight
hundred words each day on his novel *The Garden of Eden.*

Hemingway hoped to do some deer hunting while in Idaho, but his doctor advised against
it due to his high blood pressure. Hemingway would have to settle for hunting ducks.

This was Sun Valley's first mid-December winter season opening since the war. The lodge management, eager to have a celebrity writer in residence, had given Ernest and Mary a complimentary stay at the resort. But their stay was soon over and Ernest and Mary needed to look for other accommodations. They chose MacDonald Cabins in Ketchum, where they had stayed during their last trip to Idaho. They were joined there by his three sons during the Christmas holidays. Ernest rented a third cabin so he would have the privacy needed to write.

During their stay in Ketchum, Ernest noticed a black springer spaniel wandering throughout the village. On the way to his cabin one evening, he noticed the black dog continued to follow faithfully behind. The dog looked as if he hadn't eaten in days, so Ernest fed him. During the night, Hemingway found the black dog huddled close to the cabin's door trying to keep warm. Ernest brought the dog inside and the spaniel made itself at home as if he belonged there. When Ernest woke the next morning the black dog was sleeping beneath his bed. The next day Ernest inquired in the town about the dog, but no one seemed to know who owned the dog or where he came from. Ernest thought the dog was an Alaskan springer spaniel and promptly adopted him and named him Blackie (aka Black Dog). Ernest may have remembered back to a ski trip in 1926 when he and Hadley were vacationing at the Hotel Taube in Schruns, Austria. A dog named Schnauz befriended them, slept at the foot of their bed, and accompanied them on ski trips, riding on Ernest's shoulders when he skied down the hills. The dog was a good companion to their son, Bumby, and would go on walks with the young boy and his nurse, walking beside the boy's sleigh. Ernest wrote fondly about the dog in *A Moveable Feast*.

Hemingway and Schnauz in Schruns, Austria

In an article from *By-Line Ernest Hemingway* edited by William White, Hemingway reminisced about finding his beloved Black Dog in Idaho.

I thought a long time about my dog Black Dog and what the two winters must have been when he had no master in Ketchum, Idaho, having been abandoned by some summer motorist. Any small hardships we had encountered seemed to me to be dwarfed by Blackie's odyssey. We encountered Blackie when we were living in a log cabin in Ketchum and had two deer, killed, respectively, by Mary and Patrick, hung up in the open door of the barn. There was also a string of mallard ducks hung out of the reach of [the wild] cats and there were also hung up Hungarian partridges, different varieties of quail and other fine eating birds. It seeming that we were people of such evident solidarity, Blackie abandoned promiscuous begging and attached himself to us as our permanent dog. His devotion was exemplary and his appetite enormous. He slept by the fireplace and he had perfect manners.

Friend A.E. Hotchner also remembered Black Dog in his biography, *Papa Hemingway*, as a "cold, starved, fear-ridden and sub-dog in complex—a hunting dog who was scared stiff of gunfire. Ernest had brought him back to Cuba and patiently and lovingly brought up his weight, confidence and affection to the point, Ernest said, that Black Dog believed he was an accomplished author himself." Hemingway (as quoted by Hotchner) wrote that:

He needs ten hours' sleep but is always exhausted because he faithfully follows my schedule. When I'm between books he is happy, but when I'm working he takes it very hard. Although he's a boy who loves his sleep, he thinks he has to get up and stick with me from first light on. He keeps his eyes open loyally. But he doesn't like it.

Hemingway acquired most of his dogs as strays who either wandered in alone as did Black Dog one cold, wintry night in Ketchum, Idaho, or from the streets of Cuba where many abandoned dogs and cats roamed the city streets and countryside in search of food, shelter, and companionship. Ernest Hemingway usually chose his dogs and many of his cats by first impressions and an immediate connection he felt from the heart.

By late February Ernest and Mary were ready to return to warmer weather in Cuba. According to Mary, when Black Dog saw the luggage being packed into the trunk of the Buick, he climbed into the front seat of the car and would not move for fear of being left behind. But Hemingway assured Black Dog he was now part of their family and would be going home to Cuba with them.

Ernest and Mary were happy to be back at Finca Vigía, but were

Hemingway with Black Dog upstairs in the tower.

Hemingway seldom used his studio in the tower, saying he missed the company of his cats.

concerned whether Black Dog would accept their large cat family, especially Boise, and their devoted female dog, Negrita, as well as the other small Cuban mongrels Hemingway had adopted. Mary wrote in *How It Was,* "Amidst the joys and the surprises of homecoming I was concerned that our other dogs, the band of agreeable but nondescript characters who had gravitated to the Finca but lived outside the house, might upset Blackie's introduction to his new domain. Ernest had thought of that. While we were still unloading luggage and I was greeting servants and looking about, he introduced Blackie to the incumbent beasts. I noticed him following some of them around the corner of the garage, Blackie at his heels. Whatever the dog dialogue was, Blackie had to assert his authority only a couple of times before peace reigned. He was a bit bigger than any other dog, and the problem of territory never arose since little Negrita never challenged his place at Papa's feet, his realm for some twelve years. To us peripheral characters of the household he was always polite, often enchanting." Black Dog also got along well with the cats of the Finca, particularly with Boise, and settled in as if he had always belonged on the farm.

Ernest and Mary were also pleased to find the tower they had designed was finished and that several cats had already taken up residence in the cats' room off the terrace in view of Hemingway's bedroom and bathroom windows.

Hemingway spent only two weeks working in his new study on the fourth floor of the tower before he moved his typewriter back into the main house. He told Mary he missed the sounds of the house and the companionship of his cats. Black Dog was willing to climb the outside stairs to his master's fourth-floor studio, but the cats preferred the safety of the second floor terrace. Hemingway later joked with friends about how he had worked over a cat house.

Mary finally got her wish and the cats were moved to their new lodgings. But all the principal cats—Princessa, Boise, Willy, Spendy, Friendless' Brother, Good Will, and Uncle Wolfer—still had run of the house if they chose, as did Friendless. But Friendless still had a habit of spraying, and Hemingway hoped his big black cat would prefer the new cat room with its bin of catnip to entice the new residents.

The Hemingways were pleased with the completion of their new four-story tower. The first floor of the building was the carpentry shop. The second floor belonged to the cats.

The cats' room in the tower (above) was in direct view of Hemingway's bedroom and bathroom windows (opposite page), which he purposely designed so he would have a good view of his cats.

Even though closed in this recent photo, the windows to Hemingway's bedroom, study, and bath were usually open when he was there, offering easy access to his cats.

Friendless, one of Hemingway's closest cat friends, sits on the front terrace of the Finca.

chapter 21

The Cat Wars

*They fought with no noise at all:
the way they fight now. I don't
know who won.*

Islands in the Stream

By the 1950s, Ernest Hemingway not only had to deal with the death of close friends and family, but also the loss of many of his beloved cats and dogs.

The street outside the Finca could be a dangerous place for the farm's cats.

The death of his good friend and editor, Max Perkins, left Ernest deeply saddened. His mother, Grace Hall, passed away just three months before his ex-wife Pauline's sudden death. Pauline's death caused a permanent rift between Ernest and his youngest son, Gregory. The death of his publisher, Charles Scribner, came as a complete shock. Fishing pal and bar owner Joe Russell, good friend Katy Dos Passos, expatriate Gertrude Stein, and fellow writer F. Scott Fitzgerald, to name just a few, had also all passed on.

Hemingway's closest cat companions, who gave him the constant love and devotion he so desperately needed in the final years of his life, were also dying, one by one.

In 1950, Princessa—the elegant, aristocratic and most loving queen mother of the clan, according to Mary Hemingway—made herself a soft nest on top of Ernest's clothes in his cupboard and died, ladylike and elegant.

In the *New York Herald Tribune Book Review* on October 8, 1950, Hemingway discussed his writing routine and mentioned the loss of his elegant, aristocratic Persian, the first cat of Finca Vigia:

> *I work wherever I am and the earliest part of the morning is best for me. I wake always at first light and get up and start working. There is a Springer Spaniel from Ketchum, Idaho named Black Dog who helps me to work. Three cats named Boise, FriendlessBrother, and Ecstasy give valuable aid. A cat named Princessa, a smoke-grey Persian, helped me very much; but she died three weeks ago. I do not know what I will do if anything happens to Black Dog or to Boise; just go on working I suppose.*

In February, 1953, Mary found Willy, the sweetheart of the family that Ernest had adopted eleven years prior, trying to make his way back to the tower's cat room. The cat had been hit by a car, its hip shattered, and it appeared to be in shock. Mary ran

It wasn't unusual for the Finca's cats and dogs to give birth in the quiet recesses of the garage, now the offices of Museo Ernest Hemingway.

A stray dog who found a home at the Finca, possibly a descendant of Black Dog.

to Ernest for help. Hemingway gently examined their beloved pet and found that Willy was critically injured and realized there was nothing that he could do. Ernest asked houseboy Rene to cradle Willy gently in his arms while he went to get his gun. With tears in his eyes Ernest, not wanting his cat friend to suffer, pulled the trigger. Willy was buried in a small private cat cemetery, adjacent to the back terrace, next to Mary's rose bushes. That night Ernest held Mary close for a long time as they grieved for their dear cat friend. During this disturbing time at the Finca, Ernest had written in the cat's log book, a diary with detailed information about the cats' births and deaths, that several of the cats had died of distemper, other illnesses, and accidents.

Today, cats still congregate on the back terrace, next to the cat cemetery.

Friendless, the family stud cat, continued to do battle with neighboring cats that were always invading the peace and quiet of the farm. The only cat at the Finca who was a threat to Friendless was his brother Fatso, who now outweighed Friendless by at least a pound. What was once brotherly love between Friendless and Fatso had turned to rivalry. With Boise, the grandfather of the clan, aging, Fatso had become more aggressive. The fights between brothers became more serious. Ernest feared his dear cat friend Friendless might not survive the next challenge and wrote about his fears in *Islands in the Stream*:

"What about Goats?"[Friendless] "The gardener said it was not good for Goats to eat much until his wounds are healed. His wounds were severe." "What sort of fight was it?" "It was very serious. They fought for nearly a mile. We lost them in the thorn bush beyond the garden. They fought with no noise at all; the way they fight now. I don't know who won. Big Goats came in first and we took care of his wounds. He came to the patio and lay beside the cistern. He couldn't jump to the top of it. Fats came in an hour later and we cared for his wounds." "Do you remember how loving they were when they were brothers?" "Of course. But I am afraid now that Fats will kill Goats. He must weigh nearly a pound more."

Just as things seemed to be settling down at the farm, Mary found Spendy, who she said preferred cuddling and watching her type to outdoor sports, dead under a tree near the garage. The gardener told her Spendy had been killed by a male tomcat from the village, assisted by Fatso and Shopsky. Fatso's brother Friendless had also been indicted in the murder. According to Mary, a large blonde hoodlum cat had taught several of the Finca's cats to kill. Spendy was the first victim. Ecstasy, one of Ernest's early morning writing companions, was found mortally wounded and became the second casualty. Ernest knew once a cat became a killer of other cats, he would keep on killing. He knew his two beloved cats, Fatso and Shopsky, whom he had raised from kittens, would have to be destroyed, and he would have to do the deed. Mary did not indicate in *How It Was* whether Friendless, one of Hemingway's dearest cat friends, whom he immortalized in *Islands in the Stream,* suffered the same fate. It was more likely he did not survive his last fight.

Hemingway and Friendless' Brother enjoy a quiet moment together.

chapter 22

Pets, Guns, and the Pulitzer Prize

Black Dog is tired too. He'll
be glad when the book is over
and so will I.

Papa Hemingway

While fishing aboard the *Pilar* the first week of May, 1953, Ernest and Mary heard on the radio the announcement that Hemingway had won the 1952 Pulitzer Prize for *The Old Man and the Sea*. The book, about an old Cuban fisherman and his battle with a giant marlin and relentless sharks, would become one of the most enduring works of American fiction and a twentieth-century classic. Hemingway had sent close friend Marlene Dietrich the first galleys of the book. This was not the first time he had asked for her opinion of his work. According to Dietrich's daughter, Maria Riva, in her biography, *Marlene Dietrich:* "She loved the book, calling it Hemingway's Masterpiece." When Hemingway won the Pulitzer, she "went about like a proud wife who had always known her husband had even deeper greatness than was realized by those not privileged to know the real inner man."

Hemingway wrote the novella in eight weeks, energized by the youth, vitality, and beauty of nineteen-year-old Adriana Ivancich, a young Italian woman Hemingway had first befriended in 1948 when he and his wife Mary had toured Italy. Adriana, her mother Dora, and her brother Gianfranco, who would also become a close friend, visited Cuba in October 1950 as guests of the Hemingways at Finca Vigia. According to Carlos Baker in *Ernest Hemingway: A Life Story,* "Ernest liked her [Adriana's] soft voice, her rather ardent feminine manner, the evidences of her devout Catholicism, . . . and (not least) her dark beauty." She was so different from Mary, his tomboy-like wife for the past four years. Mary no longer held the same allure for him as she had in

Hemingway was captivated by Adriana Ivancich's charm.

The spacious bed offered plenty of room for Ernest, Mary, and their pets.

Hemingway with his beloved cats and dogs

1944 when, on the rebound from third wife Martha, he had been desperately lonesome for female companionship.

Hemingway's novel *Across the River and into the Trees* had been published in 1950. The book centered around an American colonel and a young Italian countess with whom he was in love. The story was inspired by Hemingway's attraction to Adriana.

Hemingway was again in love with two women, and he felt from his past relationships that it was not a sin to love both his wife and the young girl who fondly called him "Sweet Old Lion." His letters to Adriana would span a decade.

In Adriana's presence he again worked at an exciting pace. He had completed the first section of the sea book *(Islands in the Stream)* which he had not touched in three years. With his renewed energy, "the rush" as he called it, he pumped new feeling into *The Garden of Eden,* which he had started the year he and Mary were married. But it would take another love, another infatuation, nine years after Adriana with yet another young woman, before Hemingway would be able to complete the story.

Unfortunately, several incidents that happened previously that year marred the Pulitzer Prize celebration. Their beloved cat Willy, whom they had adored for eleven years, had died and they were still mourning his loss. Also, Adriana's brother, Gianfranco Ivancich, whom they had come to love as a son, left for Venice in January of 1953 to become the director of a steamship line. Gianfranco had come several years earlier for a visit, had fallen in love with Cuba and its people, and stayed on as a guest at the Finca. The handsome young Italian lived in the quarters above the cats' room in the tower. Gianfranco, a war hero and wounded veteran, was quite fond of the farm's cats and dogs, and Boise, Negrita, and Black Dog had become his close companions.

When Gianfranco departed, Hemingway felt the loss deeply. According to Carlos Baker in *Ernest Hemingway: A Life Story:* "It was worse than having somebody dead, said Ernest because a man could always reconcile himself to the 'deads' more easily than to the temporary departure of the living."

Hemingway and his wife were constantly surrounded by their cats and dogs when at home at the Finca—in the house, on the terrace, and by the pool. Also their principal cats and dogs slept with them on a king-size bed in Mary's bedroom. Hemingway captured one of these moments in *Islands in the Stream:*

> The cat, asleep on the blanket, woke as the man reached over and stroked
> him. He yawned and stretched his front legs, then curled up again. "I never had
> a girl that waked when I did," the man said. "And now I haven't even got a cat
> that does. Go on and sleep Boy."

Their little dog Negrita usually slept at the foot of the bed on Mary's side. Black Dog preferred a comfortable mat on the floor next to Hemingway, and Boise slept on Ernest's chest or by his side if he wasn't out hunting fruit rats. The other principal cats would occasionally sleep with Ernest and Mary if they found room on the big bed.

Mary in *How It Was* shared a humorous conversation she had with her husband while they were in bed one evening with their menagerie. Ernest started the conversation. " 'Black Dog—he's been dreaming about Elizabeth Barrett Browning.' 'Or about her little dog, what's its name—Ruff? Puff? Fluff?' We dozed a few minutes. Then E. said, 'Flush.' Two-thirds asleep, I tried to remember a famous Hollywood dog

Ernest and Mary relaxing down by the pool with their cats and dogs nearby

who might be the subject of Negrita's dreams, little Negrita sleeping softly on top of the bed between our feet, finally remembered and murmured, 'Miss Negrita's dreaming too. Lassie? Negrita never saw a Lassie picture.' 'No.' said Ernest, muffled in sleep. 'Rin Tin Tin.' "

But one evening in late September things turned more serious when local thieves broke into the house. Mary and Ernest felt the publicity of the success of *The Old Man and the Sea* had prompted the burglars. Mary wrote about the dangerous episode in *How It Was,* relaying how she and Ernest and their pets had luckily slept quietly through the night. If anyone had awoken, Mary felt they surely would have been killed. "The Havana papers had printed squibs about the success of *The Old Man* in the north and once again it prompted local thieves to break into the house. (Our dogs were sleeping as soundly as we were.) Avoiding our fine new booby-traps, they broke open a lock on one of our six doors and savaged the house, tearing open desk and library drawers, scattering clothes and papers around, dropping tobacco ashes and matches, spitting on the furniture. They took four of Ernest's knives, war trophies, and his gold cufflinks, ties and silver picture frames and almost all of Gianfranco's extensive, excellent wardrobe, and we observed the next morning that one of the gang had stood guard at the door to my bedroom, grinding his cigarette butts into the floor there. All of us, Ernest and I and Blackie and Negrita, had slept peacefully through the raid, to our morning-after mystification. We told the local police about it and asked them not publicize it. We did not want [Batista's] government posting guards around the Finca, especially since they might well have been in league with the thieves. We continued to sleep with pistols on our night tables, Ernest's loaded, mine empty with the cartridge clip at hand."

Mary's and Ernest's thoughts now turned toward an impending African safari. They booked passage aboard the *Flandre,* departing June 24 for Le Havre. Gianfranco would meet them, and they would drive to Pamplona, Madrid, Valencia, and then Paris before setting sail from Marseilles for Mombassa. Ernest was happy their wealthy Cuban friend and excellent marksman Mayito Menocal, the same age as Ernest's son Bumby, would be joining them on the safari, along with famed white hunter Philip Percival, who once had guided Teddy Roosevelt in 1909 and had been Ernest's and Pauline's African guide in 1933. Hemingway convinced Percival to come out of retirement to serve as the guide on the 1953 African safari. Percival was a man Ernest had immense respect for and had immortalized in his novel *Green Hills of Africa,* a fictionalized account of Hemingway's two-month safari in 1933 that combined the sport of hunting with his true personal experiences. Earl Theisen, a photographer, was hired by *Look* magazine to photograph their new adventure.

Ernest found it hard to say goodbye to Black Dog and Boise. Both animals were growing old, and both were in frail health. Hemingway was particularly worried that Black Dog did not eat well when he was away. But his houseboy, Rene Villarreal, had promised to take the dog on walks to see the cows each morning as Ernest did when he was home.

Ernest and Mary in Kenya, 1953

chapter 23

African Wildlife
and Two Airplane Crashes

. . . many of the things that had happened to her [Mary]
in hunting came as unexpectedly as being in heat for the
first time to the kitten when she becomes a cat.

True at First Light

Hemingway was excited to be back in Kenya, a country he had fallen in love with twenty years earlier. He was particularly pleased to find that Phillip Percival had received permission to hunt in the Southern Game Reserve in the Kajiado District, forty miles south of Nairobi, an area known for its abundant wildlife. In late August, they camped in the Mua Hills at Percival's farm, Kitanga, near the town of Machakos. So taken was Hemingway by the beautiful countryside that he would later name one of his adopted Cuban dogs after the town.

Ernest and Mary found it hard to say goodbye to Black Dog.

Despite the excitement of the impending hunts, Hemingway continued to miss Black Dog, dreaming of him at times and hoping he would survive until his return.

Dennis Zaphiro, the young game warden for the district where they would hunt, owned an adorable police dog puppy named Kibo after Africa's highest mountain, Kilimanjaro. Kibo was a good diversion, entertaining everyone in the camp with the energy of a puppy. Mary, in *How It Was*, described the dog as "a self-propelled ball of fuzz with tireless teeth and an appetite for everything including the tent poles."

Kibo was inquisitive and tried to make friends with a baby Grant's gazelle Zaphiro found abandoned by its mother in the tall grass. Mary immediately adopted the small creature and named him Baa because of his whispering cry. According to Mary, "Kibo the puppy rushed up to him [Baa] to investigate, [and] our stout-hearted little goat butted the puppy, who thereafter kept his distance." Ernest was so intrigued by the puppy that he told his wife he was considering adopting a police dog puppy once Black Dog passed away. Hemingway didn't want to think of his beloved dog dying, but he knew it was inevitable. His little dog Negrita had once mated with a police dog from

Souvenirs of Africa were displayed throughout the house and fascinated Hemingway's kittens.

the village, and he remembered what good dogs her puppies had become.

Hemingway would not forget the young African dog and would write about the police dog puppy in *The Garden of Eden:*

> *In the story he was waiting for the moon to rise and he felt his dog's hair rise under his hand as he stroked him to be quiet and they both watched and listened as the moon came up and gave them shadows. His arm was around the dog's neck now and he could feel him shivering. All of the night sounds had stopped. They did not hear the elephant and David did not see him until the dog turned his head and seemed to settle into David. Then the elephant's shadow covered them and he moved past making no noise at all and they smelled him in the light wind that came down the mountain. He smelled strong but old and sour and when he was past David saw that the left tusk was so long it seemed to reach the ground. They waited but no other elephants came by and then David and*

the dog started off running in the moonlight. The dog kept close behind him and when David stopped the dog pressed his muzzle into the back of his knee. David had to see the bull again and they came up on him at the edge of the forest. He was traveling toward the mountain and slowly now moving into the steady night breeze. David came close enough to see him cut off the moon again and to smell the sour oldness but he could not see the right tusk. He was afraid to work closer with the dog and he took him back with the wind and pushed him down against the base of the tree and tried to make him understand. He thought the dog would stay and he did but when David moved up toward the bulk of the elephant again he felt the wet muzzle against the hollow of his knee.

Mary was also enchanted by the African puppy, and agreed with Ernest that a police dog puppy would be a welcome addition to the farm's family of dogs.

". . . I worried about your dog."

"My dog?"

"Yes your dog in Africa in the story. I went in the room to see if you needed anything and I read the story."

. . . "It's about half through," he told her.

"It's wonderful," she said. "But it frightens me. The elephant was so strange and your father too. I never liked him but I like the dog better than anyone except you David, and I'm so worried about him."

"He was a wonderful dog. You don't have to worry about him."

"Can I read about what happened to him today in the story?"

"Sure, if you want to. But he's at the shamba now and you don't need to worry about him."

"If he's all right I won't read it until you get back to him. Kibo. He had a lovely name."

"It's the name of a mountain. The other part is Mawenzi."

"You and Kibo. I love you so much. You were so much alike."

— *The Garden of Eden*

Hemingway had read much about Africa in the months prior to their trip. He was especially concerned with the snakes of the area, some of the most deadly in the world. He wrote about the dangerous reptiles in *True at First Light:*

Neither of us were great snake hunters. That was a White Man's obsession and a necessary one since snakes, when trodden on, bit the cattle and the horses and there was a standing reward of shillings for them on Pop's farm [Philip Percival]; both cobras and puff adders. Snake hunting, for pay, was as low as a man could fall. We knew cobras as quick, lithe-moving creatures who sought their holes which were so small that it seemed impossible for them to enter them and we had jokes about this. There were tales of ferocious mambas that rose high on their tails and pursued the helpless colonists or intrepid Game Rangers while they were mounted on horses but these tales left us indifferent since they came from the south, where hippos with personal names were alleged to wander across hundreds of miles of dry country seeking water and snakes performed biblical feats. I knew these things must be true since they had been written by honorable men but they were not like our snakes and in Africa it is only your own snakes that matter.

So it wasn't surprising during a visit to see his son Patrick, living in Tanganyika, that Hemingway used extreme caution when encountering what he thought was a poisonous snake. Arriving at Patrick's farm after dark, Hemingway found his son gone and the house locked up. According to Mary, in *How It Was:* "He found a window that could be pried open, found a bed in the dark and went to sleep. He wakened with a start when something soft plopped onto his stomach from the open window, thought 'snake' and lay quiet with no muscle twitching, being a man who was not in favor of antagonizing snakes in the dark." Hemingway knew the black mamba, the most venomous snake in Africa, lived in this part of the country, a snake considered very alert and agile, a snake as comfortable on the ground as climbing a tree, a snake capable of easily slithering through the space of an opened window. Ernest also knew that a black mamba's bite usually brought death within the hour. Mary added, "Soon he thought he felt a small warmth emitting from the snake. Then it began to purr." To Hemingway's relief, a small cat had climbed through the opened window and had made itself comfortable on his stomach, sleeping in the same manner as Ernest's cat Boise did almost every evening when he was home in Cuba.

During this time in Africa, Hemingway became enchanted with a young African woman named Debba, whom he referred to as his fiancée. As with Adriana Ivancich, whom he met in Venice in 1948, he courted Debba, visited her village and her family, and showered her with gifts, all under the watchful eyes of his wife Mary. No one knows how much of the story in his memoir, *True at First Light,* is fact or fiction, but Ernest devoted the second half of his African journal to Miss Debba, the Queen of the Ngomas. Hemingway needed romance in his life to write and at age fifty-four, he may have found just that while on safari.

Philip Percival noticed that Hemingway no longer seemed interested in the kill as he had been during his 1933 safari with his wife, Pauline, and friend Charles Thompson. Hemingway seemed more interested now in observing the animals and photographing them. According to Michael Reynolds in *Hemingway: The Final Years,* "Ernest's heart was no longer in the hunt. The Finca's walls were heavy with noble, preserved heads, and he already had begun to identify metaphorically with the old trophy animals. Except for the marauding lion, [Game Warden Dennis] Zaphiro thought that Ernest was not greatly interested in hunting. "He did not, for instance, shoot or even want to shoot, an elephant. . . . He preferred to drive around and look at the animals." In fact, as soon as Menocal and Theisen left the safari, Ernest and Mary spent more time and effort observing wildlife than killing it."

Few writers have come close to

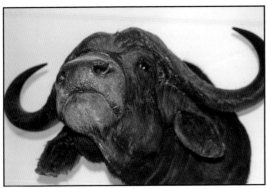

Hemingway had plenty of wildlife trophies at the Finca, but by 1953 he no longer had the urge to kill big game.

Hemingway's ability to describe Africa's wild environment. Whether it was an observant eye or that he was a hunter as well as a naturalist, he had a gift of transferring what he saw in Africa to paper and making it real.

In *True at First Light,* Hemingway wrote about a flock of vultures that were hoping to descend on a lioness' fresh kill. This passage in his African book is true poetic prose, pure Hemingway:

> *They did not look funny now though perched obscenely above the remains of the zebra and when the big lioness rose and yawned and went out to eat again two big vultures dropped as soon as she was on the meat. The young lioness flicked her tail once and charged them and they rose running and heavy winged as she slapped at them as a kitten slaps. She then lay down by the big lioness and started to feed and the birds stayed in the trees but the closest ones were almost overbalanced with hunger.*

As a belated Christmas gift, Ernest had promised Mary a low-level airplane flight along the Congo River Basin. On January 21, 1954, Ernest and Mary took off with their bush pilot Roy Marsh aboard Marsh's Cessna, stopping along the way for brief overnight stays. On January 23, while flying over the spectacular Murchison Falls, Marsh flew low to avoid a flock of white ibis and hit a telephone line, damaging both the prop and the rudder of the plane. Marsh managed to land the plane in heavy foliage. Mary broke two ribs on impact and Ernest incurred serious injury to his spine and a badly bruised right arm and shoulder. Marsh seemed to come through the ordeal almost unscathed. The trio was forced to spend the night on the side of a hill hoping someone would hear the distress calls from the airplane's radio. The next day they spotted a charter boat on the river and were rescued by the crew. Although charged an exorbitant price by the boat's captain for their trip back to civilization, they were just glad to be alive.

Bush pilot Reggie Cartwright, who was at the dock in Butiaba when the boat arrived with Ernest, Mary, and Roy on board, was among those who had searched for them in his twin engine, twelve-seat de Haviland. Although Butiaba's landing strip was only an uneven, dirt strip, Cartwright assured Ernest he had taken off from this narrow piece of land before and offered to fly Ernest, Mary, and Roy to Entebbe.

It is possible the plane was overweight with passengers, luggage, and cargo—and that Cartwright was so excited about assisting in the rescue of the world-famous author and the publicity it would bring—that he put all safety factors aside. The plane was no sooner in the air than the de Haviland came crashing to the ground. The plane's door had jammed on impact, but Roy Marsh and Mary managed to get out a small window, with the pilot Cartwright following behind. According to Michael Reynolds in *Hemingway: The Final Years,* "The right engine caught fire, igniting a ruptured fuel tank, quickly turning the plane into a death trap." Hemingway—his large, bulky frame too big to squeeze through the small window—found himself trapped in the plane, which was filling up with smoke. Despite Hemingway's injured arm, shoulder, and spine from the previous airplane crash, he managed to use his head as a battering ram to open the door. A local policeman and his wife offered the injured Hemingways and Roy Marsh a ride to Masendi, fifty miles away. After a night's stay at the Railroad Hotel, Ernest and Mary rented a car with a driver for the last hundred

The first of two aircraft crashes in Africa from which Hemingway never fully recovered

miles of their journey. In Entebbe, Ernest and Mary were put up at the Lake Victoria Hotel for a week's recuperation. On January 28, 1954, Roy Marsh arranged to fly the injured Hemingway to Nairobi aboard a Cessna 170. Mary, with Hemingway's son, Patrick, who had flown to Masendi upon hearing of the crash, arrived in Nairobi on a commercial airliner.

Hemingway had been injured far more seriously than anyone realized, including Mary. Ernest was met in Nairobi by a barrage of reporters. Refusing anything but the basic medical attention, Hemingway stayed confined to his room, easing his pain with liquor. Hemingway could tell, with the limited medical training he had gained from his father and learned firsthand from serving in two World Wars, that he had seriously injured his kidneys and possibly damaged his liver. Hemingway had also jammed a vertebra in his back during the first airplane crash, making it almost impossible to sit without pain. He was forced to either lie flat or stand to relieve the pressure. To make matters worse, Hemingway, while on a fishing trip during the last weeks of their stay in Shimoni, tried to help extinguish a brush fire and, still not steady on his feet from the injuries sustained in the airplane crashes, fell into the blaze and burned both of his arms, head, hair, and face, including his lips. On March 9, Mary and Ernest set sail on the SS *Africa* for Europe, the first leg of their journey home.

It was a total of thirteen months before Ernest and Mary saw Cuba again, and to

Hemingway's surprise, both his dog, Blackie, and his cat, Boise, were still alive and well.

When Hemingway returned home he was still seriously ill. According to biographer Carlos Baker in *Ernest Hemingway: A Life Story*, "He was still in danger of dying. Apart from the full-scale concussion, his injuries included a ruptured liver, spleen, and kidney, temporary loss of vision in the left eye, loss of hearing in the left ear, a crushed vertebra, a sprained right arm and shoulder, a sprained left leg, paralysis of the sphincter, and first degree burns on his face, arms, and head from the plane fire. With his customary pose of invulnerability he had told reporters that he had never been better. The truth was that he had never been worse. . . . He told [friend] Harvey Breit of *The New York Times* that he had twice inhaled fire before he got out of the second crash, and that this had never helped anybody except Joan of Arc."

Hemingway was glad to be home with his devoted dog, Blackie, and his dearest cat friend, Boise, by his side, and began his long road toward recovery.

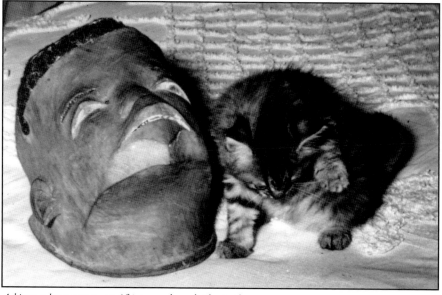

A kitten relaxes next to an African mask on display in the guest room.

Boise was constantly by Hemingway's side when he was home at the Finca.

chapter 24

Cats, Dogs, and the Nobel Prize

He [the Wolf] is hunted by everyone. Everyone is
against him and he is on his own as an artist is.

Selected Letters

Ernest woke Mary on the morning of October
28, 1954. "My kitten, my kitten, I've got that
thing . . . You know the Swedish thing."

Hemingway had won the Nobel Prize for
Literature. He was bombarded with well-
wishers and the press. Black Dog, Boise, and
the rest of the menagerie wandered among
the throngs of people who arrived at the farm
to congratulate Hemingway. The only animal
missing was Negrita, their faithful little dog
who had passed away a few weeks earlier.
According to Mary in *How It Was,* "At lunch
one day in early October, our dear little Negrita
on the floor beside me made a frightened yelp

*Hemingway was awarded the Nobel Prize
for Literature in 1954.*

and slumped sideways... I nursed her devotedly and Ernest paid her a dozen loving,
encouraging visits, but a few nights later her heart stopped." Negrita was buried in a
small grave beside the swimming pool, next to the tennis court, under the shade of a
giant ficus tree, where she and Black Dog had enjoyed many happy days. Ernest and
Mary would never forget the faithful little dog Hemingway had rescued from the
dusty streets of Havana, who had given them so much love over the years, and whom
he immortalized in *Islands in the Stream*. Adriana Ivancich wrote Hemingway, telling
him how sad she felt about Negrita's death. "I am sorry to hear about poor Negrita.
I understand her loss must have made you all unhappy? All of you, including Black
Dog."

Although Hemingway was pleased by the prestigious award, he was glad when the
whole "damn thing" was over. He had never been one to seek publicity. His work
was continuously interrupted and his privacy, which he jealously guarded, was now
being invaded by guests, many uninvited, and a barrage of press people. However, the
$35,000 check would help pay Hemingway's mounting debts. Running his Cuban farm
was not cheap. Not only did he have the expense of a sizable staff to support, but also
the responsibility and care and feeding of a large family of cats and dogs.

Hemingway worried about the health of Boise, who had recently recovered from a heart attack.

chapter 25

Boise Remembered

*Letters about the death of animals are
not the best to send.*

Selected Letters

By the fall of 1955, Hemingway still had not fully recovered from two near fatal airplane crashes in Africa the year before. By November 17, Ernest noticed that his right foot was starting to swell, caused by the infected kidney that had been damaged in the second plane crash. He had also injured his liver in the same crash. His doctor diagnosed Ernest with acute nephritis and hepatitis. By November 20, Hemingway was so sick he could only leave his bed for short periods of time.

On good days Ernest would read, write letters, and work on his African manuscript, *True at First Light,* in bed with his cats Boise, Friendless' Brother, and his dog Blackie. Boise seldom left his side, sensing the seriousness of his master's illness. Hemingway wrote about his old friend's devotion and his feelings toward his cat in *Islands in the Stream:*

> As Boise grew into an old cat, Thomas Hudson worried about the cat's health and the thought of losing his old friend was almost too much to bear. That night, when he had sat in the big chair reading with Boise at his side in the chair, he had thought he did not know what he would do if Boise should be killed. He thought, from his actions and his desperation, that the cat felt the same way about the man.

It would be January, 1956, before Hemingway felt strong enough to return to his normal routine of rising at first light to the symphony of the song birds outside his bedroom windows and the hungry cries of his cats.

Hemingway was not a big fan of movies, or their directors, and was disappointed in the making of the movie *The Old Man and the Sea* that year. Ernest felt that Spencer Tracey, a well-respected actor, had been miscast from the start as the old fisherman Santiago. Tracey had gained additional weight after being hired for the part and, to Ernest, he looked more like a fat, rich tourist than an old Cuban down on his luck. Ernest may have heard that Humphrey Bogart had been interested in making the film after reading the novel but had been diagnosed with cancer and cancelled any plans he may have had to make the movie. Humphrey Bogart would have made a more believable fisherman—not only was he an accomplished actor but he was a fine sailor who understood the sea. To make matters worse, the marlin caught for the film the previous September off the coast of Cuba were only in the four- to five-hundred-pound range, not even close to the twelve-hundred-pound fish that Hemingway had written about in his novel. There was now talk of the film crew going to the coast of Peru in

Hemingway's dearest cat friend, Boise

late April, where marlin had been reportedly caught in the thousand-pound range.

Ernest had agreed to accompany the crew as an advisor on the film, bringing with him his wife, Mary; Gregorio Fuentes, his boat captain and marlin expert; and Elian Arguelles, a friend and a skilled marlin fisherman. Hemingway was concerned about his back, which had never healed properly after his two airplane crashes in January 1954. He was now forced to write standing up. When he sat for any length of time at his desk, his herniated disk caused such pressure at the base of his spine that the pain became almost intolerable. Even alcohol now no longer dulled the pain. Hemingway's cats actually enjoyed his new writing routine, stretching out on the tall bookcase where he worked in his bedroom, in view of the open windows to the terrace and the close proximity to the lizards that frequented the grounds. The lizards that entered Hemingway's domain were immediately attacked by one of his seasoned feline hunters.

Hemingway also was concerned that his back would not be able to take the pounding of the rough seas reported off the coast of Peru. But always the adventurer, he and Mary said goodbye to their faithful dog Blackie and their beloved cats. Hemingway was concerned about the health of his feline friend Boise, who had recovered from a heart attack the previous year. Although appearing healthy, Boise had never regained the energy he had once known. Hemingway knew how excited Boise would become when he returned home, and how desperate the cat became when he sensed his master was leaving. Hemingway lovingly captured one of these moments in *Islands in the Stream:*

> Boise had been outside the house waiting for them when they had driven up in the station wagon. He had been terribly excited and had been underfoot during the unloading, greeting everyone and slipping in and out each time a door was opened. He had probably waited outside every night since they left. From the time he had orders to go, the cat knew it. Certainly he could not tell about orders; but he knew the first symptoms about preparation, and, as they proceeded through the various phases to the final disorder of the people sleeping in the house (he always had them sleep in by midnight when leaving before daylight), the cat became steadily more upset and nervous until, finally, when they loaded to leave, he was desperate and they had to be careful to lock him in so that he would not follow down the drive, into the village, and out onto the highway.

The fresh air and change of scenery agreed with Hemingway. He told friends his back was feeling stronger than ever. He even reeled in a 680-pound marlin in eight

Hemingway could see the graves of Boise and Willy from where he sat in the dining room. Note the kitten sitting on the window ledge behind the dinner guests.

minutes—the cameramen were delighted when the big fish made a dozen spectacular jumps. Ernest and Mary returned to Finca Vigia in late May of 1956, and although Ernest and Mary seemed well rested from their trip, Hemingway felt the months in Peru had been a waste of time. He would have preferred to remain at the Finca working on his African manuscript.

The Hemingways were greatly saddened when they returned home and heard the news that their dearest cat friend, Boise, had died while they were away. Hemingway would never forget his feline companion who walked with him as a dog walks, slept on his chest or by his side, sat on his lap while he read, dined with him at every meal when he was at home at the Finca, and was with him each day while he wrote. Boise had been as close to Ernest Hemingway as anyone had ever been—either human or animal—and the cat's memory would live on in the house where he had grown up as a kitten, the grounds where he chased lizards and captured fruit rats, and in the heart of

Boise was buried next to Willy in a small graveyard next to the back terrace and Mary's rose bushes. A half circle of stones still marks the gravesite where Hemingway's dearest cat friends were laid to rest.

The memory of Boise would live on in the house where he had been raised as a kitten.

Hemingway, who had written thirty-five pages about his beloved cat in his novel *Islands in the Stream.*

Boise had been buried by Rene Villarreal and the Finca staff in the small graveyard set aside for Ernest and Mary's closest cat friends. The small cat cemetery was located in view of the cats' room in the tower, Ernest's bathroom window, the library, and the back terrace where the cats would congregate in the morning and afternoon, and also in view of the dining room's double doors. The small graves were not marked, but the space was bordered by a half circle of stones and a blanket of soft green grass. Another cat graveyard was located further down the hill under the fragrant blooms of the frangipani trees. Ernest could see the cats' graves from his dining room chair. The house was full of memories of the cat he had adopted as a kitten from Cojimar and whom he called Brother.

On May 25, 1956, Ernest Hemingway wrote his dear friend Gianfranco Ivancich, knowing he would want to hear the news about Boise.

> *Boise died while we were away. I was very sorry not to be with him when he died. He died in the night and did not suffer at all. It was a heart attack and we buried him along side of Willie. Blackie [Black Dog] will not live very long either I don't think, but he still has fun and we go on walks over the property early in the morning when I wake up. . . . Letters about the death of animals are the not the best to send.*

Cristóbal and his sister Izzy enjoyed playing in Hemingway's African baskets.

chapter 26

The Next Household Cat Prince

*I have felt profound affection for three
different cats, four dogs, that I remember,
and only two horses; that is horses that I
owned, ridden or driven.*

Death in the Afternoon

Cristóbal Colón (aka Christopher Columbus), Ernest's and Mary's beloved tiger cat, became the Finca's next household princeling. Even though Cristóbal would never take Boise's place, Hemingway was quite fond of the energetic youngster and his sister, Izzy the Cat.

Izzy the Cat was usually shortened to Izzy. She was a family favorite and, according to Mary, would playfully ambush other cats by using secret maneuvers and taking advantage by attacking from high ground. She was a bold cat and much more aggressive than her brother, Cristóbal. Hemingway had first named the cat Isabella La Católica, after Queen Isabella of Spain, who, with her husband Ferdinand II, sponsored the first voyage of Columbus. The name was a tribute to the cat's adventurous nature. Cristóbal and Izzy loved to climb to the tops of Hemingway's bookshelves, playing with anything that could be moved. Hemingway's boots and African baskets became their favorite hiding places.

Hemingway's boot was a fun place to play.

The kittens' mother was named Feather Kitty. She was a shy, good-natured cat. But Feather Kitty did not like Mary, and Mary seemed to feel the same way about the cat. Mary said in *How It Was* that Feather Kitty was secretive, impatient, preoccupied and ill-tempered, although she considered her a good mother and close to her kitten Izzy. Obviously Feather Kitty did not hide her feelings about Mary, nor did Feather Kitty's mother, Thruster, Martha Gellhorn's favorite cat. She, too, disliked the last mistress of Finca Vigía. Hemingway once told his brother, Leicester, that cats show you how they feel about you.

*A cat has absolute emotional honesty. Male or female a cat will show you how
it feels about you. People hide their feelings for various reasons, but cats never do.*

Izzy was killed one evening when she ran after Black Dog's steak bone and Black Dog bit off her head. The incident was considered an accident. Izzy's mother, Feather Kitty, became despondent over Izzy's death. Ignoring her son Cristóbal, she eventually left the Finca to move in with a family outside the farm. Izzy was deeply missed by Ernest and Mary, the household staff, and Cristóbal, who missed her companionship and playfulness.

Hemingway never fully recovered from the loss of his dear companion Black Dog. He told A.E. Hotchner, "I miss Black Dog as much as I miss any friend I ever lost—I know it was all over for me here the night they killed Black Dog."

chapter 27

The Loss of Black Dog

I do not know what I will do if
anything happens to Black Dog
or Boise, just go on working
I suppose.

New York Herald Tribune Book Review

In 1957, Ernest and Mary were still mourning the loss of Boise and Negrita. Then Hemingway's faithful spaniel Black Dog [Blackie] was murdered by the soldiers of Cuba's dictator, Fulgencio Batista, sending Hemingway into a deep depression. According to Ernest's brother, Leicester, in his biography *My Brother, Ernest Hemingway:* "That black springer spaniel [had] lived in the house and regarded himself as a watchdog's watchdog, just as Ernest was a writer's writer. Over the years he came to love Ernest as more than a master. He regarded him as the center of existence. He quietly mourned when Ernest went on trips. He ate well only when the master was in residence. When Ernest slept, Black Dog guarded the entrance door. When Ernest swam, Black Dog waited beside the pool. When Ernest went to the tower

Hemingway never fully recovered from the loss of his spaniel Black Dog.

workroom, Black Dog climbed the steps and waited to come down with him. Ernest said Black Dog had learned the relationship between typing and food, for Ernest always worked first and ate afterward. He said he sometimes fooled the dog by typing a letter in the afternoon. By the mid-fifties, Black Dog's eyesight was failing. He had learned to track lizards by smell instead of sight. In a letter to Harvey Breit, Ernest confided that Black Dog had suffered a wonderful near miss recently. A lizard had been on a chair, and Blackie had tracked him expertly with his nose on the yellow tiles, while the lizard admired him. Finally Blackie located the chair but still had not seen the lizard on its arm. Ernest told him to look up and he would see the lizard. Just as Black Dog looked up, the lizard leaped clear over him, but the dog made a beautiful snap at him in midair. This, Ernest said, was the classical type of near miss that the establishment specialized in. Black Dog was still deadly on moths and flies because of their steady movement. It was frozen motion that baffled his tired eyes. Black Dog hated the police and military, but Ernest said he worried about the dog's inability to distinguish

135

Black Dog was buried beside Negrita in the area where they once played.

between the Salvation Army and the Guardia Rural. As the Castro guerilla warfare spread in eastern Cuba, life in and near Havana grew increasingly tense. A nocturnal search for arms out at the Finca resulted in a show of loyalty by Black Dog. For this he was struck in the skull by a rifle butt and killed instantly. Ignoring the urgent advice of everyone, Ernest went into Havana and formally lodged a complaint against the search party who had wantonly struck and killed his faithful dog. The protest was duly noted by the Batista government. Though no action was taken, Ernest maintained enormous public respect."

Hemingway never completely recovered from the loss of Black Dog. According to Carlos Baker in *Ernest Hemingway: A Life Story* "Black Dog had died at the Finca and Ernest turned more morose than ever at the 'dull fight' he was having to make." Hemingway believed dogs and cats had souls. According to Valerie Hemingway in her autobiography *Running with the Bulls: My Years with the Hemingways,* "As far as he was concerned, his Black Dog was up there in heaven with all the faithful, if he wasn't, it was not a place Ernest wanted to be. I never knew what extent he was being serious when he made remarks like that, but I think at the time for him was the truest statement he ever made."

All through the spring of 1957, Ernest continued in a depressed state. Trying to cope with the loss of Black Dog, Hemingway wrote to friend and poet Archibald MacLeish, who he knew owned animals himself:

> Me I'd trade all the honours in the world for two good bottles of Claret a day and to have my Black Dog back again young and well and not buried down at the pool alongside the tennis court.

After Black Dog's untimely death Hemingway remembered back to a few years earlier, to an adorable German Shepherd puppy named Kibo that had befriended him while on safari in Africa. Hemingway may have felt a police dog would have the physical stamina to stand up to the raiding parties of Batista's army. His Black Dog—elderly, almost blind and deaf—never had a chance. Ernest decided to adopt a police dog from the village and named him Machakos after the town in Kenya's lion country where he had hunted big game with Mary and famed white hunter Philip Percival. Juliette Cunliffe in her book *The Encyclopedia of Dog Breeds* writes that German Shepherd dogs (police dogs) derived from old breeds of herding and farm dogs, were used as war dogs and used later in police and security work. The breed was attentive, loyal and courageous. Hemingway was looking for a young dog with these traits. However, the new dog, although younger and stronger than Hemingway's Black Dog, had no defense against the guns of Batista's soldiers. According to Carlos Baker in *Ernest Hemingway: A Life Story*, "At four o'clock one morning in August [1957] the rougher side of politics came uncomfortably close when a government patrol entered the grounds of the Finca, looking for a fugitive from the rebel underground, and killing Ernest's new dog Machakos. With an effort he kept silent, but it was one more instance of the perils of living under a dictatorship."

Hemingway wrote his good friend Gianfranco Ivancich January 7, 1959, informing him of the latest news on his dog Machakos, happy to have at least received some type of retribution:

> *The sergeant (the bisco . . . from Cottorro who came on the robberies) who killed Machakos our dog and tortured several of the boys of the village was hanged a couple of months ago by the boys of Cottorro with the usual mutilations.*

Although Ernest Hemingway had won a Pulitzer Prize in 1952 for *The Old Man and the Sea,* and the Nobel Prize for Literature in 1954—two of the most prestigious awards a writer could wish to obtain—these honors were overshadowed by his declining health, the loss of so many of his friends (human and animal) and the instability of the country he had called home for twenty years.

Hemingway wrote Adriana Ivancich (undated): *Cuba is not lost. It has only changed masters.* But, in his heart, he knew Cuba would never again be the same.

Hemingway with his beloved friend Black Dog.

Hemingway would never fully recover from the loss of his dearest animal friends.

chapter 28

Two Cats and an Owl

Planned to train him. Maybe
make him think he's a falcon.

Papa Hemingway

Boise and Black Dog were still in Hemingway's thoughts when he and Mary visited Ketchum, Idaho, in the fall of 1958, for a much needed vacation and change of scenery. Hemingway had found Black Dog abandoned and half starved in this town ten years earlier. Despite seeing old friends, Ernest could not stop missing his animal friends.

Mary and Ernest loved the small western town with its wood boardwalks, panoramic views of the mountains, and close proximity to the Sun Valley ski resort. It was an enchanting place where they could relax, and where Ernest continued to write well.

A.E. Hotchner, visiting Hemingway and Mary that fall, felt the cool mountain air agreed with his good friend, and he wrote about Hemingway's appearance in *Papa Hemingway.* "I couldn't believe his metamorphosis. He had become taut, the slack was gone, the smile back, his eyes were clean, the old timbre in his voice, and ten years had left his face. He was alive with enthusiasm and plans." Ernest was writing well. He continued to work on his novel *The Garden of Eden,* fueled by the passion he felt for two women in his life, Adriana Ivancich and Marlene Dietrich, loves that had never been consummated. According to Steven Bach in *Marlene Dietrich: Life and Legend,* "Hemingway wrote Dietrich into *Islands in the Stream* (as Thomas Hudson's beloved wife, "the good general") and into *The Garden of Eden.*" In Hemingway's African journal, *True at First Light,* Ernest referred to Dietrich as his "beautiful non-existent wife."

Hemingway showed Hotchner a notebook in which he had written about his Paris days with first wife Hadley, and said he was considering publishing a book of his Paris sketches *(A Moveable Feast).* Hotchner was one of Hemingway's closest friends, a young writer Ernest had met in 1948. On October 4, 1949, Hemingway wrote his publisher, Charles Scribner, saying, "I really trust Hotchner." He was a true confidant and one of the few people from whom Ernest sought literary advice and trusted to edit his work since the 1947 death of his editor, Max Perkins. Throughout their fourteen-year friendship Hemingway allowed Hotchner "to photograph him and to take notes of their conversations." Hemingway may have felt Hotchner would write the truth, and tell a good story. In 1966, five years after Ernest Hemingway's death, A.E. Hotchner published his biography *Papa Hemingway.* It became an instant bestseller.

The weather was perfect in Idaho that season. Hemingway wrote in the mornings and hunted in the afternoons. The only thing missing was the companionship of his cats and dogs back in Cuba.

Late that October, Ernest and Mary were pleasantly surprised when they found two kittens left on the steps of their rental cabin, gifts from young friends. Mary wrote about them in *How It Was.* "On Halloween we found on our doorstep a present from neighbor children—two gray-and-white striped kittens, brother and sister, weaned but still wobbly. We welcomed them with warm cream and more sophisticated tidbits, nests by the fire and floods of affection, and after they had explored all our corners and smells and settled in comfortably, we found the boy cat, Big Boy Peterson, to be one of the great charmers of his tribe, sweet-natured, witty, stout-hearted, loving, trustful, entranced with the movement of water running from the faucet. The girl cat, Sister Kitty, proved to be Big Boy's opposite. She was self-centered, suspicious, mean-tempered and a bore, but we put up with her because we felt Big Boy might like a companion in the hours we were away, prowling around in sagebrush." Ernest enjoyed watching the two energetic kittens as they romped through the cabin. Big Boy Peterson reminded Ernest of his cat Cristóbal back at the Finca.

Ernest and Mary named the great horned owl Owlry.

One day while Hemingway was bird hunting with friends he winged a young great horned owl that had been sitting in a tree. Ernest had been taught the skills of animal doctoring by his father. He examined the injured creature and decided to take the owl back to his cabin and try to repair the damaged wing.

In a barn behind the rented cabin, Ernest built a box with a perch for the young owl. He and Mary named the bird Owlry. According to A.E. Hotchner, Ernest trapped mice for the owl and also gave him the heads of ducks and rabbits he shot. As the owl's wing began to heal, Ernest considered training the owl in the ways of a falcon. There was no doubt Hemingway had a way with animals, even wild ones.

One morning he and Mary discussed the freshness of a piece of elk's liver. Hemingway decided the owl would make the final decision. When the owl refused to eat the meat, the liver was then given to their cats Big Boy Peterson and Sister Kitty. Hemingway wrote his son Patrick on November 24, 1958, from Ketchum, Idaho, about their trip and his plans for the future. He also included a drawing of the owl:

> It has been wonderful here since we drove out October 6 . . . . Write 4 days a week—hunt 3 and sometimes afternoons if go well. . . . We are living in a cabin near the creek but have to shift to another December 20th—can shoot ducks till Jan 6th—I want to finish book [A Moveable Feast] here— go back to Finca— straighten up various things, situations income tax and then go to Spain for San Isidro and stay there during the summer. Then would like to go out to Africa in the fall. . . . Cuba is really bad now, Mouse. I am not a big fear danger pussy but living in a country where no one is right—both sides atrocious—knowing what sort of stuff and murder will go on when the new ones come in—seeing the

Good friend and hunting companion Forrest "Duke" MacMullen with Owlry and Hemingway.

Ernest and Mary's last home in Ketchum, Idaho, overlooking Big Wood River

Big Boy Peterson was fascinated by the movement of water in the kitchen sink of the Ketchum house.

abuses of those in now—I am fed up on it. We are always treated OK as in all countries and have fine good friends. But things aren't good and the overhead is murder. [Cartoon of owl head] Unsuccessful great horned owl kuss (Have one in barn.)

Ernest and Mary enjoyed their stay in Ketchum and, uncertain about their situation in Cuba, they decided to buy a house. The Dan Topping house was a modern home, built on the side of a hill with a breathtaking view of the mountains and the trout-filled waters of the Big Wood River.

At the end of their stay that season Hemingway decided to release the owl, as his wing had completely healed, taking him back to the tree where he had been found. But, according to A.E. Hotchner, the bird had bonded with Ernest and had different thoughts, following Hemingway back to his car. The second time Hemingway took the owl to the tree, the owl again flew back to the car. Hemingway was forced to take the bird back to the barn. Ernest knew none of his Ketchum friends would be willing to adopt the wild creature because he had been the only one who had been able to make friends with the owl. It was finally decided the bird would once again be taken back to the tree by his friend Duke MacMullen, but this time Ernest would not accompany the bird. If the owl could not see Ernest it was hoped he would stay perched on the tree, and he did.

Ernest loved to travel by automobile. He particularly enjoyed riding in a convertible so he could see the countryside and the wildlife, keeping a diary of the creatures he saw along the way. When he and Mary decided it was time to drive south, back to their home in Cuba, they made arrangements with friends to look after their house and their two cats, Big Boy Peterson and Sister Kitty, who had become loving members of their family.

On arrival in Cuba on March 29, 1959, they were pleased to find their farm was in good shape, the staff cheerful and, as Mary wrote in *How It Was,* "the pool deliciously clean and cool, the house fresh and airy, beasts healthy, vines, shrubs, flowers and trees flourishing." Hemingway was particularly glad to see his cat, Cristóbal, whom he had missed.

Hemingway loved to travel by convertible in order to view the wildlife. He kept a diary of the animals and birds he saw on his trips.

Cuban friends gave their views of the revolution. Despite the fact the economy was in decline with private construction now at a standstill, the people of Cuba were still hopeful. Hemingway may not have felt the halt to the unbridled construction a bad thing. High rises were being built everywhere. There was even talk of dredging in the bay in front of the Malecon, Havana's famous scenic waterfront drive, to make room for more hotels. Thoughts of Havana governed by Batista's corrupt brother, Panchin, and the U.S. organized crime boss, Meyer Lansky, were bad enough, but the possibility of it becoming another Miami Beach was something Hemingway didn't want to think about. Hemingway wrote Gianfranco Ivancich, January 31, 1958, about his fears of overdevelopment:

> *Will try to remember news. The tunnel is finished and will be opened in February they say. They are now talking of filling in the bar from Maine Monument to the Castillo de La Punta to make more land to build Hotels on. The present Malecon to be an inside street . . . Havana is more like Miami Beach all the time. I do not know where to go. Do you?*

Havana skyline

Ernest and Mary's visit to their Finca Vigia home was short. They flew to New York on April 22, 1959, for some last-minute shopping before boarding the SS *Constitution* April 26 for Algeciras. Hemingway wanted to update his book *Death in the Afternoon* and had planned a summer trip to Spain to follow the bullfighting circuit. Hemingway loved Spain almost as much as he did Cuba. The villa where they were staying in Malaga, owned by old friend Bill Davis, was surrounded by pines, palms, acacia trees, flowering plants, and vines. It must have reminded Ernest and Mary of their beloved Cuban farm and the animals they left behind in the care of Rene Villarreal and the old man Mundo, caretaker of the cows. According to Mary, "Rene was a quiet, intelligent, well-mannered young man of seventeen" when she was first introduced to him by Ernest. The boy lived with his family in a small house outside the farm and had been hired by Hemingway to help care for his large family of dogs and cats. "He was gentle and kind with the animals," Mary said. Now in charge of managing not only the animals, but the farm, Rene, promoted from houseboy to butler, had become a close and trusted friend. Ernest and Mary were sure their Cuban farm was in good hands.

Hemingway's thoughts often turned to his farm in Cuba. Ernest and Rene Villareal are shown observing new litters of kittens and puppies in front of the Finca's garage, a safe haven for the newborns.

Big Boy Peterson enjoying a bright sunny, wintry day in Ketchum, Idaho

chapter 29

"Your Big Kitten" in Cuba and Spain

I love you dearest kitten.

Selected Letters

Ernest and Mary returned to Cuba in January 1960. Hemingway had agreed to write a long article on bullfighting for *Life* magazine. He always wrote well in the confines of his Cuban home, surrounded by his cats and dogs. The loving memories of Boise and Black Dog were always close at hand. Ernest's secretary, Valerie Danby-Smith, who was nineteen and whom he had met the previous year in Spain, where she had assisted him in his work, arrived in late January to help. The Finca staff fell under the spell of the young Irish girl, presenting her with a black, furry kitten named Pelusa. Smith, who was staying in the guest house next door to the main house, referred to her cat as "uncomplicated company." By April, Hemingway had written 63,000 words for the *Life* article entitled *The Dangerous Summer*. According to Carlos Baker in *Ernest Hemingway: A Life Story:* "he complained that his contract with *Life* had been nothing but a headache, he seemed to have forgotten that they had asked for only 10,000 words. He alone had insisted on expanding it. By May 28, he declared it finished at 120,000 [words]." Hemingway felt he needed to return to Spain to gather up loose ends, despite the fact he had pushed himself beyond his limits both physically and mentally to finish the

Above: A recently adopted Finca kitten looks out from the second-story balcony of the guest house.
Below: Valerie Danby-Smith stayed in the casita (guest house) while in Cuba.

piece and was showing the first signs of a physical and mental breakdown. This time Hemingway would make the trip alone. Mary had chosen to stay behind. She felt the previous trip to Spain had been a disaster, with their constant bickering taking a toll. She would meet him in New York at their small East Sixty-Second Street apartment on his return in the fall. Hemingway's secretary, Valerie, planned to meet him in Europe at a later date. Like Adriana Ivancich (also nineteen when the two first met), the young Irish girl may have become the new inspiration Hemingway needed for the character,

Marita, in his novel, *The Garden of Eden.*

"I'm your girl," she said in the dark.

"Your girl, no matter what I'm always your girl.

"Your good girl who loves you."

Attracted by Valerie's youth and gentle charm, Ernest may have found himself again in love with two women. In Valerie Hemingway's autobiography *Running with the Bulls: My Years with the Hemingways,* Valerie said that Ernest Hemingway fantasized about having a life with her. He talked about marriage and having the daughter he had always wanted. According to Valerie, Ernest had asked her to come to Cuba, telling her that he was considering suicide (due to his declining health), and only her presence by his side made life worth living. Valerie wrote in her book that Ernest said he loved her and always would.

The Garden of Eden, which he began in 1946, took a new turn (1959–1960). The passion he now felt for Valerie may have inspired this passage.

> *He was happy to be alone to have finished his work for the day. Then the loneliness he always had after work started and he began to think about the girls and to miss them; not to miss the one nor the other at first, but to miss them both. Then he thought of them, not critically, not as any problem of love or fondness, nor of obligation nor of what had happened or would happen, nor of any problem of conduct now or to come, but simply of how he missed them. He was lonely for them both, alone and together, and he wanted them both.*

Hemingway became infatuated with Valerie Danby-Smith, possibly his last true love.

According to biographer Carlos Baker in *Ernest Hemingway: A Life Story,* when Hemingway arrived in Madrid his friends were surprised to find only the shell of the man they had seen on his previous trip in 1959. Baker wrote: "He showed the symptoms of extreme nervous depression, fear, remorse, loneliness, ennui, suspicion of the motives of others, insomnia, guilt, remorse and failure of memory." Hemingway was experiencing the same type of paranoia that his father had suffered from in the last years of his life before his suicide.

Hemingway had also become disillusioned with the bullfighting circuit, whether it was from his declining health or the fact he felt the sport that he had loved and had consumed so much of his life was now corrupt. Ernest wrote his wife Mary in August complaining about his physical and mental health:

*Kittner I don't know how I can stick this summer out. Am so damned
lonesome and the whole bullfight business is now so corrupt and seems so
unimportant and I have so much good work to do. . . . Only this, I am afraid
of, no, not only this, is complete physical and nervous crack up from deadly
overwork. . . . Would have given anything to have pulled out of here as soon as I
saw how things were. Honey, I miss you so and our old lovely life. . . . I loath this
damned bull business now and I want to clean my work up and get the hell out.*

According to Carlos Baker, Ernest wrote Mary repeatedly, calling her "poor blessed
kitten" and saying he now realized why she had hated Spain so much in the summer of
1959. His declining health had taken its toll. He wished that she was with him now to
keep him from "cracking up." Despite the fact that they had drifted apart and that their
marriage had deteriorated to the point that Mary had threatened Ernest with divorce,
he missed her strength and her ability to keep his life organized and focused. It wasn't
unusual for Hemingway to sign his letters to his wife "Your Big Kitten" during times of
stress. Any reference to cats was usually comforting to him.

Hemingway was so depressed that he remained in bed his last few days in Spain before
departing for New York. Valerie planned to visit Ireland before returning to New York,
but she promised Hemingway that when she returned to the United States she would
remain in New York City in case he needed her. After a brief stay in New York, Ernest and
Mary took the train to Idaho. Mary hoped that the town of Ketchum, close friends, and
his beloved cat, Big Boy Peterson, would be enough to rally Ernest once again.

Big Boy Peterson and Hemingway enjoying a meal together at his home in Idaho.

When in Idaho, Hemingway missed his cats and dogs in Cuba, especially Cristóbal.

chapter 30

Without His Cats

How people cling to their
useless lives I do not understand.

Portrait of Hemingway

It was clear to Mary and their close friends
in Ketchum, Idaho, that Ernest was in need of
medical attention due to his depressed state of mind.
Surprisingly, he still continued to write well, although
he said he missed his extensive reference library
and his cats and dogs in Cuba, especially Cristóbal,
who had become a close companion. By November,
Ernest's blood pressure had reached an alarming
rate of 250 over 125, and his paranoia seemed to be
escalating. It was decided by Mary and Ernest's close
friend and doctor, George Saviers, that Hemingway's
problems were psychological, despite the fact he was
fighting a losing battle with kidney and liver disease.

Cristóbal joined Hemingway at each meal.

He also had type II diabetes, which may have been partly responsible for his erratic
behavior and dark moods, according to his niece, Hilary Hemingway, in her article,
"The Hemingways and Diabetes." It was arranged that Hemingway would be registered
at the Mayo Clinic at St. Marys Hospital in Rochester, Minnesota (where Ernest's
father had once attended classes). Dr. Hugh R. Butt, a liver specialist, was Hemingway's
physician at the clinic. Dr. Howard Rome, who had limited knowledge of Hemingway's
lifestyle, diet, or medical history, was one of two senior consultants of psychiatry at
the clinic. Under confining conditions, and away from his pets, Hemingway's blood
pressure continued to rise at an alarming rate. His doctors decided his depression was
being caused by the very same drugs that Ernest was now taking to control his blood
pressure. Misjudging the situation, they took him off his blood pressure medication.
Dr. Rome found that this action not only did not release Hemingway from his
depressed state of mind, but his doctors were aware that his mental condition became
significantly more severe. To make matters worse Dr. Rome prescribed, and personally
administered, a series of controversial electric shock treatments, despite the fact that
Hemingway had suffered a severe concussion six years prior.

Hemingway was now being forced to deal with confinement, the absence of family
and pets, and the horrors of shock treatments at a rate of two per week. A man who
lived to write, and needed to write to live, was now being subjected to a medical
treatment known to erase a person's memory, taking away the one thing Hemingway

Hemingway's Idaho cat, Big Boy Peterson, kept the writer company while he worked.

needed to live a functional life.

According to Dr. Marty Becker in *The Healing Power of Pets* "medicine is recognizing the special relationship between pets and people as one of the most powerful weapons in fighting disease and treating chronic conditions. In fact, many doctors are [now] routinely 'prescribing' pets for their patients."

Hemingway's cats and dogs had guided him through some of the loneliest times of his life and comforted him when he was depressed or ill. This time Hemingway did not have his pets by his side to ease the pain both physically and mentally. He missed his cat, Big Boy Peterson, who remained in Ketchum. He missed his sons, whom he seldom saw anymore, although he and Patrick, now living in Africa as a professional hunter, continued to correspond regularly. He missed lovely Valerie. Her presence had given him "the rush" as he called it, the energy he needed to write. And, surprisingly, he missed his wife, Mary, whom he still fondly called Kitten. He also worried about his farm in Cuba and his cat, Cristóbal, but he knew his butler, Rene, would take good care of his home, staff, and pets.

When Hemingway was released from the hospital and arrived home, according to Carlos Baker in *Ernest Hemingway: A Life Story,* "There was a curious distance behind his eyes. Sometimes he stood gazing from the wide front windows across the river towards the Ketchum cemetery through the boughs of the leafless cottonwoods. He seldom spoke of what he saw, if indeed he was seeing anything. . . . Except for very occasional letters, he wrote nothing—Ernest would sit there . . . saying pitifully that he could not write—it just wouldn't come anymore. Tears went coursing down his cheeks."

To make matters worse, according to his son, Patrick, after the April 15, 1961, failure of the Bay of Pigs invasion in Cuba, Hemingway was informed by the F.B.I. that he would not be allowed to return to Cuba. This was devastating as it meant that he could not go back to his farm, his boat, his library of nine thousand books, his paintings, his unfinished manuscripts, and his family of dogs and fifty-seven cats. On April 21, Ernest Hemingway attempted suicide with a gun. After a second attempt on April 23, Mary decided she had no choice but to readmit Ernest to the Mayo Clinic. There, Dr. Rome, whose medical treatments were already known to have affected Hemingway's memory and ability to write, was once again administering the same debilitating shock treatments. According to Valerie Hemingway in her autobiography *Running with the Bulls: My Years with the Hemingways,* the United States government in 1960 had expressed their wish that Hemingway, one of Cuba's most high-profile residents, cease living in Cuba and openly voice his opposition to Castro's government. Washington hinted Hemingway could be branded a traitor if he did not comply. In the past, Hemingway had ignored threats from the United States government. Cuba was his home. He was a writer. The political problems in Cuba were not his concern. Hemingway had seen many governments come and go in Cuba since 1932. He could not fathom the thought of leaving his home of twenty years. He was too old, his health was failing, and he could not bring himself to think of the consequences. He considered the Finca staff and his cats and dogs his family. However, this time the United States government meant business, and Ernest and Mary would not be allowed to return to their Cuban home. Hemingway's life, as he knew it, was now over.

Cats had always comforted Hemingway when he was lonely or depressed. Cristóbal was a loving companion.

chapter 31

"Good Night, My Kitten"

The way he and Boise felt now, he thought, neither one
wanted to outlive the other.

Islands in the Stream

"Good night, my kitten" were the last words
Ernest Hemingway ever spoke to Mary on the
evening of July 1, 1961.

At age sixty-one, with his Idaho cat Big Boy
Peterson by his side, Hemingway—knowing he
would never again smell the sweet wild grasses
of Africa, see the blue-green waters of the Gulf
Stream, or the white-capped mountains of
Idaho—took his own life in the same manner
as he had taken the kudu, the cape buffalo, the
leopard, and the lion.

*The Ketchum home where Ernest took
his life on Sunday, July 2, 1961*

> *I was happy that before he died he had lain down on the high yellow rounded
> mound with his tail down and his great paws comfortable before him and
> looked off across his country to the blue forest and the high white snows of the
> mountains. —True at First Light.*

In the morning, Sunday, July 2, Mary awoke to the sound of a shotgun blast and
found her husband lying dead on the floor of the front foyer of their Ketchum house.
Mary first told the press that the shooting had been an accident, saying later it was
months before she could face the truth that Hemingway intentionally killed himself.
Mary knew if Hemingway's death had been ruled a suicide, the Catholic Church would
have denied him a Catholic burial.

Hemingway's son Patrick had a different view of his father's death than that of his
stepmother. In a statement published in Tillie Arnold's 1999 biography *The Idaho
Hemingway,* Patrick Hemingway said, "I believe it was criminal not to have taken the
easy things away from him. I'm looking at it from the standpoint of a tough-minded
cop. I don't believe in the virtuous widow theory. No way should the investigation of
his death been as simple as an inquest."

When Marlene Dietrich received word of Hemingway's death, she wore black and
locked herself in her room reading Ernest's letters over and over. According to her
daughter, Maria Riva, in *Marlene Dietrich,* her mother "played widow. . . . She never
really came to terms with her friend's death nor ever forgave him for deserting her. She
secretly blamed his wife. 'If I had been there with him he would never have done it.'"

The theory that Mary, who may have feared Hemingway was going to divorce her, had intentionally left the keys to Ernest's gun cabinet out where he could find them—knowing he was not only suicidal, but had already attempted to kill himself twice before—has been debated continuously since Hemingway's death. Also, Mary knew Ernest's will in Cuba left everything to her.

Hadley Mowrer and her husband, Paul, were fishing in Wyoming when Hadley received the news. She had last written Ernest on May 14, less than two months before his death, signing the affectionate letter "Cat," a name Ernest had fondly called her when they were living in Paris. According to Gioia Diliberto, in her biography, *Hadley*, "she was always grateful to Ernest for giving her a belief in herself, . . . 'the key to the world,' she said. She cherished the memories of him. But, after a time, she never wavered from believing that their divorce had been for the best."

Martha Gellhorn understood why a man she had once loved chose to take his own life, especially after watching her mother die a slow, agonizing death from cancer. Caroline Moorehead in her biography *Gellhorn: A Twentieth-Century Life* wrote, "When Hemingway committed suicide, she did not blame him for not wanting to 'stay around for a long rotting finale. . . .' In public she continued to remain aloof about Hemingway . . . saying the gross inaccuracies, inventions and exaggerations written about him were his own fault. . . ." In a letter expressing her dislike of his widow, Martha called Mary Hemingway "one of the historical maggots who feed off the dead."

Adriana Ivancich had already grieved once, in 1954, for Hemingway when she heard that he had died in a plane crash in Africa. She had taken to her bed, hysterically crying and reading and rereading his letters to her. When the Hemingways docked in Venice after the ordeal, Ernest and Adriana had a tearful reunion at the hotel, with Hemingway pledging his continuing love for her. Adriana's brother Gianfranco, who was staying as a guest at the Idaho house at the time of the suicide, attended Hemingway's funeral.

Sara Murphy wrote to Ernest at the Mayo Clinic on May 24, concerned about his health. He had been there for her when she lost both of her teenage boys from illnesses

Sara Murphy

in the 1930s. Hemingway had been close to both sons, Baoth and Patrick, and was especially fond of Patrick. He felt their loss deeply and may have expressed his grief in his novel *Islands in the Stream* when Thomas Hudson hears the news about the deaths of his two sons in a tragic car accident.

He thought that . . . he could come to some terms with his sorrow, not knowing, yet that there are no terms to be made with sorrow. It can be cured by death and it can be blunted or anesthetized by various things. Time is supposed to cure it, too. But if it is cured by anything less than death, the chances are that it was not true sorrow.

According to Sara Murphy's daughter, Honoria Murphy Donnelly, in her book *Sara and*

Gerald: Villa America and After, Sara's husband Gerald had written a friend on July 10th concerned about how Sara was dealing with the death of Hemingway. "Sara is repairing slowly, . . ." Gerald wrote. "Ernest's death effects her deeply. . . . She had written him . . . assuming that his illness would pass that it was unlike him to be ill. . . . He always warned us he would terminate any such situation."

Tillie Arnold and her husband Lloyd met Hemingway in 1939 when he first arrived in Sun Valley. Tillie and Ernest were constantly together that season and a close friendship was formed. She loved Ernest and he adored her. Tillie said that she was sure that Hemingway did not want to kill himself but she felt Hemingway no longer believed he could be the man he wanted to be. He became more withdrawn. His health was deteriorating rapidly. It was obvious that he was losing the fight.

William H.A. Carr wrote in *The Basic Book of the Cat,* "The end of a dear friend can never be anything but a time of sorrow, and none of us likes to look ahead to that day. But endless processes of life and death cannot be denied, and it is better for death to find us prepared than to close our eyes and ears and minds to the inevitable fate that awaits us all."

Hemingway and Castro only met one time, in 1960.

chapter 33

Fidel Castro and the
Last of the Finca Cats

He is one of the greatest authors that ever lived.

Fidel Castro, in
Hemingway in Cuba

Several days after Ernest's funeral on July 5, 1961, in Ketchum, Idaho, Mary was contacted by Cuba's minister of foreign affairs. The Cuban government wanted to know what Mary's plans were for Finca Vigia and indicated they were interested in preserving the house as a museum. The farm was already showing signs of neglect due to the lack of money coming into the estate to maintain the farm. Also, Mary had received a disturbing phone call from her butler, Rene Villarreal, telling her bookworms had invaded Hemingway's library. Mary knew Fidel Castro grew up reading the works of Hemingway and was an admirer of her husband. She felt that the Cuban government's sentiment on turning their home into a museum was sincere.

It was obvious that Castro's government could appropriate the Finca at anytime if they so desired. They had already taken control of many of Cuba's finest homes and businesses. But Castro was making an overture to Mary out of respect for Ernest Hemingway. Castro knew Hemingway had considered himself a Cuban and called Cuba his home. Mary knew that United States citizens were now prohibited from traveling to Cuba. After Hemingway's death, Mary sought help from President John F. Kennedy, who also deeply admired her husband, and professional advice from her and Ernest's attorney, Alfred Rice. Rice advised Mary to do what she could to recover Hemingway's manuscripts and possibly their art collection. Luckily, Mary was able to pull all the right strings, and the U.S. Immigration authorities in Miami agreed to give her and Ernest's secretary, Valerie Danby-Smith, exit and reentry permits for Cuba.

To Mary's surprise, the Finca Vigia was still intact, and the beautiful red, orange, and purple flowers of the bougainvillea vines that she and Hemingway loved were in full bloom. Roberto Herrera, Ernest's part-time secretary and brother to José Luis Herrera, Hemingway's Cuban doctor and close friend, had been appointed the caretaker of the Finca by the new government. José Herrera, a staunch supporter of the revolution, had been named chief of the medical division of Fidel Castro's army. Roberto immediately came to the Finca to pay his respects. Mary was overwhelmed by the task of sorting out Ernest's personal papers and asked Roberto for his assistance.

The Finca's staff, as well as Hemingway himself, had been supportive of the revolution. Batista's overthrow of the Cuban government in 1952 had spelled tragedy for the island nation and opened the doors to U.S. organized crime rule under mob boss Meyer Lansky. According to Hugh Thomas in his book, *Cuba: The Pursuit of Freedom,* "Batista's golpe in 1952 was incredible, an event comparable in the life of an individual to a nervous breakdown after years of chronic illness." On March 27, 1952, the United States ambassador to Cuba, Willard Beaulac, arrived in Havana to meet with Batista's new foreign minister. The United States had given recognition to Batista's corrupt regime. According to Carlos Baker, in *Ernest Hemingway: A Life Story,* "As an old student of revolutions, Ernest took the position that any change in Cuba was better than none. Batista's gang had looted the rich island naked, and Ernest estimated that they had made off with $600 to $800 million. . . . 'I wish Castro all the luck,' said Ernest. 'The Cuban people now have a decent chance for the first time ever.' His only regret was that Hemingway had not been on hand to see Batista pull out."

Hemingway had told Mary that he thought seventy percent of the island's population had supported the revolution with Castro promising the poor free health care, day care, and education for their children, as well as better housing and a monthly allotment of food. Castro kept his promises to the poor, bulldozing down the slums outside the cities where babies died at birth from lack of medical care and where children were forced into prostitution to help feed their families. But when Castro turned toward communism and Russia for help, Hemingway was devastated.

Mary was pleased to find that Cristóbal, the household princeling cat she and Ernest had been so devoted to and had dearly missed while in Ketchum, was still alive and well, but all the cats and dogs were a little thinner due to a shortage of food at the farm. Mary remembered how, as a kitten, Cristóbal would climb up Ernest's pants leg to his shoulders, fascinated with Ernest as he wrote, attacking Ernest's pencil as it moved across the page. Like Boise, Cristóbal dined with Ernest at each meal, eating cooked shrimp, fish, and lean meats. Cristóbal's favorite food was corn on the cob, especially a half-eaten cob that Ernest would hold in his hand while Cristóbal dined. Mary remembered a day Cristóbal turned up missing. She and Ernest had looked everywhere, fearing the worst. Three days later Mary opened her dresser drawer and out climbed their gentle, loving cat. From then on she and Ernest agreed they would always leave their dresser drawers and closets open with just enough space that their cat could come and go. But, due to Mary's long absence from the farm, the cat had now grown distant. Mary wrote in *How It Was,* "Cristóbal, who had been my day and night constant companion, had developed a new life in the pantry and among the servants downstairs, greeted me politely, as a visitor but rebuffed my gushing advances." But, according to Valerie Danby-Smith Hemingway in *Running with the Bulls: My Years with the Hemingways,* when she and Mary were reestablished at the Finca, Cristóbal took his rightful place on the dinner table to the right of where Hemingway once sat, "eyes closed as he purred contentedly. When the aroma became too much for him to bear, he sat up straight and stared till some diner was hypnotized into forking over a tasty morsel. . . ." (Valerie married Ernest's son Gregory in 1966.)

While sorting out her husband's papers, which seemed an unending task, according to Mary in *How It Was,* she received a call from Fidel Castro's aide. Mary was told that the Cuban prime minister would be arriving the following day to extend his condolences to her. Mary assembled the Finca's staff and told them they would give Fidel Castro a royal welcome. The cats and dogs would also have to be on their good behavior. Mary knew if she was going to be able to remove Ernest's manuscripts from Cuba, she would need Castro's approval. Castro arrived in the early evening, without fanfare. This was the first time he had visited Hemingway's house, although this was a man and a writer he greatly admired. Castro may have been told by Dr. José Luis Herrera that Hemingway had supported the revolution. Dr. Herrera also knew Hemingway had held Batista's army personally responsible for the brutal murders of his dogs, Blackie (Black Dog) and Machakos.

Castro, with Cuban Minister of Culture Abel Prieto, tours Hemingway's home at Finca Vigía in 2003, walking past the pool where Ernest had spent many relaxing days.

In the Finca's spacious living room, adorned with Hemingway's African trophies and his collection of art, Castro walked towards a comfortable chair on the far side of the room. Mary mentioned that that particular chair had been her husband's favorite. Castro paused but Mary invited him to sit. She was hoping Castro would offer his assistance. Several cats, including Cristóbal, may have watched the stranger with curiosity. The cats missed their master with his gentle voice. The man in the green army fatigues was tall and bearded like their master and walked with the same air of authority, but Hemingway would have stopped to talk to them, calling each one by its name. The stranger sitting in their master's chair kept his eyes focused on Mary.

Castro may have sensed the frustration Mary was feeling, overwhelmed by the immense challenge that lay ahead of her. According to Mary in her autobiography *How It Was,* he invited her to remain at the Finca. "Why don't you stay here with us in Cuba," Castro said. Mary graciously declined, knowing full well the United States government would never allow such an arrangement. She told Castro that there was much to do in the United States, handling her husband's estate. But Mary did ask him if he would retain her employees at the Finca, and he agreed. He also told Mary that he would leave the guesthouse untouched in case she decided to return. Castro kept his promise. The cozy two-story guesthouse, with the view of the Finca's gardens, looks the same today as it did the day Mary left Cuba for the last time. Before leaving the Finca, Castro toured the house, spending a few minutes gazing into Hemingway's bedroom, where Ernest once stood and wrote, and his study with his desk piled high with stacks of mail, his slippers still next to his bed, a pair of glasses and a visor on the night table. It was hard for anyone to imagine Hemingway would not be returning.

The cats followed Castro throughout the house, sitting on the open window ledges and the bookcases as they had done when their master was at home, giving him, as he said, "valuable aid." Castro, intrigued by the four-story building off the terrace, asked to see the tower. Walking past dozens of cats that had congregated outside the

The Cats' Tower at Finca Vigia

cats' room in the tower and several small dogs with curled tails, Castro climbed the outside staircase of the tower to the patio on the roof as Hemingway had done so many mornings with Black Dog following faithfully behind. As Castro and Mary stood looking at the panoramic view of the countryside, according to Mary, Castro said, "I imagine Señor Hemingway enjoyed this view." "Every day," Mary said.

Mary distributed checks to her longtime employees, gifts, she told them, from Ernest. Gregorio Fuentes, Hemingway's boat captain, was given all of Hemingway's fishing gear and the ownership of Hemingway's beloved boat, the *Pilar.* Mary had asked Fuentes to take the boat out and sink her, but Gregorio knew Ernest would have never approved of the request. Fuentes was not able to afford the upkeep of the boat, which had been turned into a work boat, and donated the *Pilar,* Hemingway's most prized possession, to the Cuban government. By then, the boat was in desperate need of repairs. After extensive renovations, the thirty-eight-foot Wheeler yacht was put on display at the Finca, on the grounds of the tennis court next to the graves of Hemingway's dogs Negrita and Black Dog. The boat, now restored to its original beauty, sits as a magnificent reminder of Hemingway's exciting deep-sea adventures.

Rene Villarreal received the most generous sum for his seventeen years of devoted service. Villarreal's kindness to their dogs and cats was also well known. Rene had applied for a job with an iron works company in a nearby town, never dreaming there would be a job available at the Finca after Hemingway's death. But the Cuban government, on hearing of his longtime friendship with Ernest, offered Rene the position as the first official curator of the Finca Vigia, one of the many reasons why Hemingway's home stands almost undisturbed today, just as he left it more than forty years ago. Unfortunately his other homes have not been kept as Hemingway left them. The Key West, Florida, home was stripped of most of the furniture, books, and mementos before being placed on the market for sale; his possessions in the house in Ketchum, Idaho, were also not preserved in their entirety.

But according to Gladys Rodriguez Ferro, the director of Hemingway Studies at the Institute of Journalism in Havana, despite Villarreal's dedication to preserving

Hemingway's legacy, after Hemingway's death many of Ernest's letters, boxes of negatives, and photographs were taken without permission, as were some personal items. "We trusted people who were not trustworthy," Ferro said.

It was hard for Mary to say goodbye to her home, which held so many wonderful memories, to the cats she and Ernest had called love sponges and purr factories, the pack of small dogs with the curled tails that Ernest referred to as his Cuban mongrels, and to her devoted staff at Finca Vigia, who had been like a family to her for the last fifteen years. Although Mary had given generous sums of money to her Finca staff, she made no long-term provisions for the support of the Finca's fifty-seven cats or the farm's family of dogs. Due to the lack of food at the Finca, the cats were forced to hunt fruit rats, lizards, and birds to supplement their meager rations. The remaining dogs at the farm were given scraps of food by the Finca's staff, but as the supplies of food dwindled there was not enough food to sustain them. The dogs grew thin, and some became sick with disease from lack of medical attention. According to Gladys Rodriguez Ferro, due to the short supply of food at the Finca and throughout the country during these troubled times, there was little to feed the large number of cats at the Finca and, one by one, the cats, descendants of Princessa and Boise, left the farm in search of food and the loving care and companionship they once knew.

As of this writing, three stray cats and two dogs have taken up residence at the Finca and are being cared for by museum staff members who unselfishly bring food from home. Due to the United States' continued embargo against Cuba, it is still a luxury to own a pet. The new cats have been christened Gregory, Mary, and Hilary.

It has been said that if you see a black-and-white short-haired cat with a black mask over his face, a silver-gray Persian with golden eyes, or an Angora tiger cat roaming the Cuban countryside, it could be a descendant of one of Hemingway's Finca Vigia cats—particularly if it has a taste for fresh chilled mangoes or corn on the cob.

The Cast of Cats

The place is so damned big it doesn't really seem as
though there were many cats until you see them all
moving like a mass migration at feeding time.

Selected Letters

He started to climb again and at the top he fell and lay for some time with the mast across
his shoulder. He tried to get up. But it was too difficult and he sat there with the mast on his
shoulder and looked at the road. A cat passed on the far side going about its business and the
old man watched it. Then he just watched the road.
—The Old Man and the Sea

Ambrose—A black and white short-haired Cuban cat who, according to Mary Hemingway, suffered from neurotic spells and lacked a sense of humor. Known as the kitchen cat, Ambrose outlived Hemingway by eight years and was sixteen years of age when he died in 1969. (aka Ambroses, Ambrosio, Ambrose Bierce)

Bates—A favorite Cuban kitten of Hemingway's son, Gregory. Ernest wrote his son, Patrick, in 1942, that he was sorry Bates had died. He told Patrick it was the same illness (distemper) that had killed the kitten's brother, Pony. The kitten may have been named after Bob Bates, the Red Cross captain and inspector of ambulances who was Ernest's close friend in Italy.

Big Boy Peterson—One of two kittens Ernest and Mary found on the doorstep of their rental cabin in Ketchum, Idaho. According to Mary, Big Boy Peterson was considered a sweet-natured, witty, stout-hearted, loving, trustful cat, one who was entranced with the movement of running water. He was the brother of Sister Kitty, who was a good companion to her sibling. Big Boy Peterson and Hemingway became close friends and, as did his cat Boise, kept him company while he wrote. He dined with Ernest at each meal, and slept with him every night. Big Boy Peterson would rise with Hemingway at first light—and was probably the last one to see Ernest Hemingway alive.

Blindie—The name of two Cuban kittens that were born blind. The two females were the daughters of Martha Gellhorn's favorite cat, Thruster. Boise, Thruster's father, was also the father of her kittens. Martha felt the inbreeding was the cause of the kittens' blindness and had all the adult cats at the Finca sterilized.

Boise—A Cuban black-and-white short-haired cat with a distinctive black mask over his face. Boise was Ernest Hemingway's dearest cat friend, adopted as a kitten from Cojimar and named after the cruiser *Boise*. Boise mated with Princessa, and thus began the Finca cat family. Boise was devoted to Hemingway, slept with him almost every night, kept Ernest company while he wrote, and dined at each meal, eating whatever Hemingway ate. Boise disdained other cats, considering himself a human. The cat also took long walks with Ernest, usually at first light. Boise was Hemingway's closest cat friend, whom he immortalized in his novel *Islands in the Stream,* devoting thirty-five pages to his beloved cat. Boise was fourteen years old when he died from a heart attack. Hemingway was deeply saddened when he heard the news of his cat's death and was sorry he couldn't be with Boise when he died. Boise was buried in a private cat cemetery next to Willy, beside the back terrace at Finca Vigia and Mary's beautiful rose bushes. Hemingway would never forget his closest cat friend, whom he called Brother. Hemingway believed cats had souls and that he would see Boise in heaven. (aka Dillinger, Dingie, Boy, Boysy, Boissy D'Angelas)

Catherine Tiger—One of Hemingway's favorite cats when he was growing up in Oak Park, Illinois. Ernest christened the strong-willed feline Catherine because of her independent nature, and possibly named her after one of his favorite historic female figures, Catherine the Great. In later years, Hemingway would name two strong female characters in his novels Catherine, a name he may have associated with the historic woman figure he had admired as a child.

Crazy Christian—A favorite Cuban kitten black as night who dined with Hemingway each morning. He was as fast as light and had a tail that was a plume that scampered with him. He was gay hearted, young and handsome. He knew all the secrets of life. He was killed by the bad cats from the village. Ernest, saddened by Christian's death, wrote a poem about his beloved, small feline (see next page).

To Crazy Christian

There was a cat named Crazy Christian
Who never lived long enough to screw
He was gay hearted, young and handsome
And all the secrets of life he knew
He would always arrive on time for breakfast
Scamper on your feet and chase the ball
He was faster than any polo pony
He never worried a minute at all
His tail was a plume that scampered with him
He was black as night and as fast as light.
So the bad cats killed him in the fall.

Ernest Hemingway

Cristóbal—An adorable tiger cat that was spoiled from much loving. His sister was Izzy, and his mother was Feather Kitty. He adored people and showed little interest in other cats. The cat's playful nature soon brought Ernest and Mary under his spell. Cristóbal became the principal cat after Willy, Princessa, Friendless, and Boise passed away. He regarded himself as the household princeling. He ate at the dinner table with Ernest at each meal, as had Boise. His favorite food was corn on the cob, which Hemingway would hold in his hand and feed to the cat. Cristóbal kept Hemingway company while he wrote and, when bored, the cat would climb onto Ernest's shoulders to get a better view. Hemingway was quite fond of Cristóbal, although he would never take the place of Boise. When Mary left Cuba for the last time, Cristóbal stayed behind. He, as Mary put it, "had taken up with members of the Finca's staff." (aka Christopher Columbus, Cristóbal Colón, Stobbs)

Ecstasy—The third brother of the Cuban triplets that included Spendy and Shopsky. Thruster was their mother. Willy, one of the Finca's favorite cats, taught him pigeon stalking, which he enjoyed, spending many hours in the tall grass stalking birds. A gentle, loving cat, Ecstasy kept Ernest company in the early morning hours while he worked. Hemingway's son Gregory was fond of Ecstasy and nicknamed him Smelly, a name he may have earned because he was a cat who liked to investigate everything by smelling it first. Ecstasy was killed by a hoodlum tomcat from the village. (aka Smelly)

-F-

Fatso—A beautiful, big, black cat that was one of the principal stud cats in the Cuban cat family, an honor he shared with his brother, Friendless. Princessa was his mother, and Boise was his father. His three other siblings included Furhouse, Thruster, and Friendless' Brother. Hemingway loved the big black cat and wrote about him in *Islands in the Stream*. As an adult, he became the rival of his brother, Friendless. Fatso was taught to kill Finca cats by a village hoodlum cat and sadly had to be put down by Hemingway, who had raised the cat from a kitten. (aka Fats)

F. Puss—A big, loving, Persian cat with large yellow eyes, who was given to Ernest's son, John (Bumby), by Hadley's good friend, Kitty Carnnell. F. Puss would babysit Bumby in Paris when the femme de ménage was away and would not allow anyone to come near the boy. F. Puss kept Hemingway company as he wrote in the early morning hours, and Hemingway wrote about his son's Paris cat in *A Moveable Feast*. (aka Feather Puss)

Feather Kcat—A kitten adopted by Ernest and his first wife, Hadley, when they moved to Toronto, Canada. The cat became Hadley's constant companion in the last month of her pregnancy while Ernest was away on assignments for the newspaper. When Ernest and Hadley left for Paris, Feather Kcat was given to close friends.

Feather Kitty—A pale gray-and-white-striped Cuban cat that was considered secretive, impatient, preoccupied, and ill-tempered, according to Mary Hemingway. She had two kittens—Izzy the Cat and Cristóbal—and was considered a good mother. She was close to Izzy, despite Feather Kitty's disagreeable personality. When Izzy was accidentally killed, Feather Kitty became irritably despondent and eventually left the Finca, moving in with a family outside the farm.

Friendless—A Cuban cat Hemingway described as a big-shouldered, heavy-necked, wide-faced, tremendous-whiskered, black fighting cat. One of the principal stud cats at the Finca, Friendless was a cheerful cat who loved Hemingway, but who had to take second place to his father, Boise. His siblings included Friendless' Brother, Fatso, Furhouse, and Thruster. When he had the opportunity, Friendless would take walks with Hemingway, and he slept with him on occasion. Friendless was one of

Hemingway's closest cat friends, known to drink whiskey and milk with his master. He was immortalized in *Islands in the Stream*. Friendless defended the farm from marauding toms from the village, but it is believed did not survive his last fight. (aka Bigotes, Big Goats, Goats)

Friendless' Brother—A Cuban cat that was thought to be a male when born, but turned out to be a female. Her mother was Princessa, and her father was Boise. Thruster, Furhouse, Friendless, and Fatso also came from the same litter. Hemingway said Friendless' Brother was an unfortunate cat who had many sorrows and occasional ecstasies. She was a quiet cat that adored Hemingway. She sat with Hemingway while he wrote and occasionally slept with the writer when Boise was out hunting fruit rats. Hemingway mentioned the friendly feline in *Islands in the Stream*. (aka Bro)

Furhouse—A Cuban cat featured in *Islands in the Stream*. Just as was Willy and Friendless, Furhouse was addicted to catnip. His mother was Princessa, and his father was Boise. He came from the same litter as Fats, Friendless, Friendless' Brother, and Thruster.

-G-

Good Will—A beautiful, long-haired, Cuban Angora tiger cat from Guanabacoa who was given to Hemingway as a Christmas gift from a local fisherman. Hemingway named the cat as a tribute to Nelson Rockefeller. Good Will enjoyed the attention he received from Ernest's sons, Patrick and Gregory. He particularly enjoyed performing circus tricks for Hemingway on the Finca's front terrace. He had the run of the house and enjoyed posing for photographs, particularly in Ernest's favorite living room chair. He was extremely photogenic, and there are numerous photographs of Good Will in the Finca's photo collection, many taken by Ernest himself. The cat was mentioned in *Islands in the Stream*. (aka Will)

-I-

Izzy the Cat—An energetic female tiger cat whose brother was Cristóbal and whose mother was Feather Kitty. Like most of Hemingway's cats' names, this one's name was shortened. Her Cuban name, Isabella, became Izzy. Hemingway had named the cat Isabella after Queen Isabella of Spain who, with her husband, Ferdinand II, sponsored the first voyage of Columbus. The name was a tribute to her adventurous nature. She was a bold cat and much more aggressive than her brother. Izzy was accidentally killed when she went after Black Dog's steak bones. She was terribly missed by Ernest, Mary, the Finca staff, and her brother, Cristóbal. (aka Izzy, Isabella la Católica, the queen)

Littless Kitty—A beautiful, black, friendly Cuban cat known for her loud purrs and her enjoyment of catnip. She was a favorite of Hemingway and he featured her in *Islands in the Stream*. (aka Nuisance Value)

Manx—One of Ernest's childhood cat friends in Oak Park, Illinois. Manx earned his name after getting his tail cut off in a door. Ernest's father, Dr. Clarence Hemingway, administered first aid and the cat, minus his tail, recovered.

Miss Kitty—An energetic black-and-gray-striped kitten with a face like a pansy. She was the daughter of a wild tiger cat that lived in a barn behind Ernest's and Mary's rental cabin in Ketchum, Idaho. The Hemingways adopted the spirited creature and were entertained by her adventures during their stay in Idaho. When their vacation ended, Miss Kitty joined Ernest and Mary for the car ride east. The cat was adopted by the Hemingway's friend, Didi Allen, whom they were visiting in Murray, Utah.

Mooky—A male stud cat Hemingway befriended out West that had the courage to battle a badger and survive.

Pelusa—A small, black, furry kitten given to Valerie Danby-Smith, Hemingway's secretary in Cuba, by the Finca Vigia staff on her saint's day, March 17, in 1960. Valerie, who was staying in the Finca's guest house, referred to her kitten as "uncomplicated company." When Smith left Cuba, the staff promised to look after the gentle feline until her return.

Pony—A Cuban kitten, the brother of Bates. They were both diagnosed with distemper. Ernest doctored them, but the disease soon killed both kittens.

Princessa—First named Tester by Ernest and third wife, Martha, she was renamed Princessa by the Finca's household staff because of her elegant nature. Hemingway purchased her from the Silver Dawn Cattery in Miami, Florida. She was a fine-boned and delicate smoke-gray Persian with yellow eyes, reminding Ernest of his son's Paris cat, F. Puss. Princessa kept Ernest company while he worked, giving him, as he said, "valuable aid." She adored Hemingway, but became mean and distant with everyone else. Princessa mated with Boise and became the grandmother of all cats at the Finca Vigia. Hemingway immortalized her in his novel *Islands in the Stream*. (aka Tester, Baby)

Shopsky—A Cuban cat, the brother of Spendy and Ecstasy. Mary and Ernest first named him Shakespeare, but felt the name was a great burden for such a small kitten. They changed his name to Barbershop, eventually shortening it to Shopsky. Friendless taught him the skill of hunting lizards and fruit rats, plentiful around the Finca. A hoodlum tom cat from the village taught Shopsky to kill Finca cats. Sadly, it was decided Shopsky, whom Ernest was fond of and had raised from a kitten, would have to be put down by Hemingway. (aka Shakespeare, Barbershop)

Sir Winston Churchill—A brooder that ignored the playful advances of other cats. The Cuban cat spurned milk and cream, but was not turned off by fish or chicken Hemingway had marinated with alcohol.

Sister Kitty—One of two kittens left on the doorstep of Ernest's and Mary's rental cabin in Ketchum, Idaho, by neighborhood children. Her brother was Big Boy Peterson. Although Sister Kitty was self-centered, suspicious, mean-tempered and a bore, according to Mary, she was considered a good companion for her brother.

Snowball—A white polydactyl Key West cat given to Hemingway in 1931 when he lived on Whitehead Street by boat captain Stanley Dexter.

Spendy—The son of Thruster and brother to Shopsky and Ecstasy. Spendy was a sweet, gentle Cuban cat that became Mary Hemingway's shadow and loving companion. The third member of the black-and-white triplets was a true love sponge and purr factory who preferred cuddling with Mary to spending time outdoors. Spendy was known to drape over Mary's books while she was typing or stretch out on the breakfast table next to Mary, keeping her company while she drank her coffee. Spendy was killed by a marauding tom cat from the village. (aka Stephen Spender, Spendthrift)

Stranger—A soft, brown-furred descendant of Princessa. She was a delicate creature, fragile of mind and body.

-T-

Taskforce–One of the Cuban cats, mentioned in *Islands in the Stream,* who loved the results of catnip, as did Friendless' Brother, Littless Kitty, and Furhouse.

Thruster—A Cuban cat, she was Martha Gellhorn's favorite feline and her constant companion while she worked on her novel, *Liana.* Thruster's mother was Princessa, and her father was Boise. Unfortunately, in her first heat, Thruster mated with Boise. The results were two kittens born blind. When Martha left to report on the war in Europe, Thruster became mean and distant, partly because the next mistress of Finca Vigia, Mary Welsh, refused to make friends with the lonesome feline. (aka Thrusty)

Uncle Wolfer—The son of Princessa and Boise. A close cat friend of Ernest, Uncle Wolfer had inherited the delicate sensibilities of his Persian mother and was included in the principal Cuban cats of Hemingway's novel, *Islands in the Stream*. Uncle Wolfer was a conservative cat, not adventurous like Boise. He disdained anything new, including catnip. He was a long-haired cat and smoke-gray, like his mother. Because of his beautiful gray coat, Hemingway referred to the cat as the Snow Leopard. Uncle Wolfer was devoted to Hemingway, and, although timid, he enjoyed being trained to do circus tricks on the front terrace to please his master. (aka Wolfer, Uncle Wolfie, Stoopy, Stoopy Wolfer)

-W-

Willy—A beautiful gray-and-black-striped cat that Hemingway wrote about in *Islands in the Stream*. According to Mary, he was a "banker type" who believed he was not a cat. He was a square businesslike cat that, according to Mary Hemingway, disdained most cats, but liked people. Known for his loud purr and gentle nature, he was a favorite cat of Ernest's sons, Patrick and Gregory. Willy liked catnip, which made him purr even louder. He loved to be picked up, cradled, and to have his stomach stroked. Willy was definitely a people cat who was deeply loved by Ernest and Mary. In his eleventh year, Willy was hit by a car and his injuries were so severe he had to be put down by Hemingway. He was deeply mourned by Ernest and Mary and the Finca staff. Willy was buried in a private cat cemetery set aside for Hemingway's most beloved cats. (aka Willie, Uncle Willy)

The Cast of Dogs

Black Dog—An Alaskan springer spaniel abandoned in Ketchum, Idaho, that Hemingway adopted. The dog followed Ernest home and was sleeping outside in the cold when Hemingway found him. Black Dog became devoted to his master, and Hemingway thought of him as his dearest dog friend. Hemingway's love for him ran so deep that he feared for the time when this dog would die of old age. Black Dog slept at his feet while he wrote or read and never left Hemingway's side when he was home at the Finca. This close relationship lasted ten years before Black Dog was murdered, clubbed to death by Batista's soldiers. He was buried in a private dog cemetery next to the pool where he spent many relaxing, lazy days with his master by his side. According to biographer Carlos Baker, Hemingway never recovered from the loss of Black Dog. Hemingway believed dogs had souls and that Black Dog was in heaven and that he would soon see him there. (aka Blackie)

-C-

Chickie—A dog owned by Paxtchi Ibarlucia, a jai alai player who was Ernest's close friend and occasional tennis partner. Paxtchi was a frequent visitor to the Finca and always brought along his dog, Chickie, a playmate of Negrita's mentioned in *Islands in the Stream*.

-K-

Kibo—A young police dog puppy befriended by Ernest and Mary when they were on safari in Africa. The energetic youngster was named after Africa's tallest mountain, Kilimanjaro, and was owned by game warden Dennis Zaphiro. Mary referred to Kibo as a self-propelled ball of fuzz. Hemingway was so taken by the puppy he considered adopting a police dog when his beloved Black Dog died. Hemingway wrote about the young African dog in his novel *The Garden of Eden*.

-L-

Lem—A Cuban pointer puppy whose mother was Negrita. His father was a pointer from the village. Lem grew into a large, loving dog who, at times, was said to be "too affectionate." Hemingway wrote about the pointer in *Islands in the Stream*. Due to Lem's rambunctious nature, his visits inside the house were limited.

-M-

Machakos—A Cuban police dog Hemingway adopted after Hemingway's beloved dog, Blackie (Black Dog), was murdered by Batista's soldiers. The dog was named after a town in the lion country of Kenya where Ernest and Mary had hunted on safari. Machakos was also killed by Batista's soldiers, deepening Hemingway's depression.

-N-

Negrita—A small black and white female dog with a curled tail, which Hemingway described in *Islands in the Stream* as having "tiny feet, . . . delicate legs, . . . a muzzle as sharp as a fox terrier, . . . eyes loving and intelligent." Negrita reminded Hemingway of Wax Puppy, a dog he and first wife Hadley had owned in Paris. Hemingway rescued the little dog from the streets of Havana, in front of the Floridita. She became one of Ernest's and fourth wife Mary's closest dog friends. When she passed away due to a heart attack, she was buried in the dog cemetery next to the Finca's pool, under the shade of a giant ficus tree.

-S-

Schnauz—A dog who befriended Ernest and first wife Hadley while they were vacationing at the Hotel Taube in Schruns, Austria. The dog slept at the foot of their bed and would accompany them on ski trips, riding on Ernest's shoulders when he skied down the hills. The dog was also a good companion to their son Bumby and would go on walks with the young boy and his nurse, walking beside the child's sleigh. Ernest would fondly remember the dog in *A Moveable Feast*.

-T-

Tassel—A white Yorkshire terrier owned by Hemingway's grandfather Ernest (Abba) Hall. The Hemingway family lived with Hall during the first years of Ernest's life, and Ernest became extremely fond of the small dog.

-W-

Wax Puppy—A puppy Hemingway gave Hadley in Paris during the last months of her pregnancy. Wax Puppy had an adorable personality and a tail that curled up on his back. The dog died of an incurable disease while Ernest and Hadley were away in Toronto, Canada. Hemingway would never forget the small dog, and he would become known for adopting dozens of small, stray dogs with curled tails in Cuba that reminded him of his beloved Paris puppy.

Other Animals

Cotsies Pride—A Cuban milk cow given to Hemingway as a gift by his friend Mayito Mencoal. Ernest named the small cow Cotsies Pride (Cotsies was a nickname Ernest had for his cats). Ernest would tell friends the cow gave seven liters in the morning and seven more at night. Ernest had calculated that the milk cow would save the farm $44.60 a month on milk, and when the cow calved, would give them double the milk. The farm's cats were served milk at each feeding. Cotsies Pride was a welcome addition to the Finca's menagerie.

Owlry—A young great horned owl in Ketchum, Idaho, that Hemingway winged while out bird hunting. Hemingway rescued the injured bird and took it back to his cabin to repair the damaged wing. The owl bonded with Hemingway, and when the bird was ready to be released, refused to leave his new master. It took three trips to the forest before the owl decided to remain in the woods.

Hemingway with his pet owl Owlry whom he planned to release into the wild.

Acknowledgments

I would like to thank my daughter, Shamlene (Shamie) Kelly, a devoted animal lover who was the heart and soul behind this book. Her typing of this manuscript alone made this book possible. I cannot thank her enough for her hard work and support. Thanks, too, to my husband, Terry Brennen, for his help throughout this eleven-year labor of love. His proofing of my manuscript and his suggestions were greatly appreciated. Special thanks to June and David Cussen of Pineapple Press for believing in this book, and for June's expert editing, patience, and always pointing me in the right direction. I'd also like to thank Pineapple Press editorial assistant Helena Berg for all her help, which was greatly appreciated; production manager Shé Hicks for her beautiful design of the book; and Tom Nordblad and Alisha Herrington for their help. Many thanks to my dear friend Scott Martell, one of the best editors I know. His help also in editing, designing of the book, and photo placement was invaluable, and I could not have done this book without him. Thanks also to Michael Gulnac, who spent many hours scanning the photographs in this book. Many of these historic photographs were in need of extensive restoration. His expertise in this field, and recommendations for cropping of photographs, was greatly appreciated.

A special thanks to Hilary Hemingway for the foreword to the book, her valuable advice, believing in this book from conception, and most of all for her friendship. And thanks to her husband, author Jeff Lindsay, whose knowledge of the Spanish language kept me pointed in the right direction while I was in Cuba, and he always made me laugh. I would also like to thank my good friend and author Randy Wayne White, who has always believed in me.

I would like to thank Megan Desnayers, Deborah Leff, Hemingway Curator Susan Wrynn, and Stephen Plotkin of the Hemingway Collection at the John F. Kennedy Presidential Library in Boston for their help and support. I would also like to thank Allan Goodrich, Maryrose Grossman, Jessica T. Sims, and a special thanks to James Hill of the audiovisual archives at the John F. Kennedy Library. This book could not have been completed without their extensive help and knowledge. A special thanks to Lydia Zelaya at Simon & Schuster for her advice, patience, and assistance. Her help was invaluable. Also I'd like to thank Scott Schwar, past executive director of the Ernest Hemingway Foundation of Oak Park, and Dr. Luis Vasquez, of both MILA Tours and Golden Airlines, who helped make my research trips to Cuba memorable.

I'd like to acknowledge for their interviews and insights Dr. Sandy Spanier, Penn State University; Scott Donaldson, biographer and past president of the Ernest Hemingway Foundation; Prof. J. Gerald Kennedy, Vice President of the Hemingway Society; Dr. James Nagel, the University of Georgia; Jenny Phillips, Max Perkin's granddaughter, and her husband, Frank Phillips; and Dr. Jack Crocker of Florida Gulf Coast University.

For granting the use of transcriptions of interviews with Hemingway scholars and President Fidel Castro, I'd like to acknowledge WGCU Public Media at Florida Gulf Coast University and Dr. Kathleen Davey. I'd also like to thank Sheri Coleman and Tim Kenney of WGCU for their assistance in Cuba. Thanks also goes to Gail Morchower, librarian of the International Game Fish Association's Fishing Hall of Fame Museum in Dania Beach, Florida.

I am especially grateful to the Cuban Hemingway scholars whose interviews gave me new insight into Hemingway's life and his relationships to his cats and dogs. To the Finca staff members who worked for Ernest Hemingway and shared their memories with me, I owe a great debt.

To President Fidel Castro, for his thoughts on Hemingway's life, although his use of me as a human shield while walking down the stairs of the Finca in 2003, was not in my best interest. I later learned there have been over six hundred attempts on his life. The man, although in his late seventies, is still sly as a fox.

I would like to thank the following individuals in Cuba for their aid in this project: Abel Prieto, Cuban Minister of Culture; Marta Arjona, director of the Cuban National Heritage Council; Gladys Rodriguez Ferrero, the director of Hemingway Studies at the Institute of Journalism; Manual Sardinas Gonzalez, the director of Museo Ernest Hemingway; and the Research and Conservator staff members at Finca Vigia: Francisco Echevarria Valdes, Maria Caridad Valdes Fernandez, and Alberto Isaac Perojo. Thanks also to Raul Chagoyen and Amparo Gonzalez Menendez, whose help was greatly appreciated. Amparo is also an excellent artist who paints beautiful portraits of cats and who feeds the stray cats at the Finca Vigia with food from her home.

I'd also like to thank Danilo M. Arrate Hernandez for his insight and friendship and Esperanza Garcia Fernandez, historian at Hotel Ambos Mundos, for her help. I'd like to thank Denise Jacques, the wife of the Canadian ambassador to Cuba, who opened her home, the former estate of Jane and Grant Mason, to us and allowed me to tour and photograph the home. Through Denise I gained a greater understanding of Jane Mason.

A special thank you to Hemingway's captain, Gregorio Fuentes, for his gracious interview, a memory I will keep forever. And to Majel Reyes Iuesada—I can't thank her enough for all her help, humor, and her beautiful smile. And to our driver, Philip, thank you for your service and patience.

I'd like to thank Dr. Carol and Patrick Hemingway for their help and kindness, particularly for Patrick's interview, and for Carol and Patrick's help on my Key West chapters. And for the insight gained from interviews with Hemingway family members, I'd like to thank Dr. Sean and Dr. Colette Hemingway, Angela Hemingway, Mina Hemingway, John Hemingway, Valerie Hemingway, John E. Sanford, Dr. Gregory Hemingway, and Carol Hemingway Gardner.

I would like to thank Hunter Johnson and Kenwood "Woody" Yow at Getty Images. Their research was greatly appreciated. And thanks to Anne-Lie Rosenquest at Tiofoto in Stockholm, Sweden, for her help and patience.

I'm grateful for the research assistance of my dear friends and antique experts Sandy and Johnny Simpson. Their knowledge of historic books and magazines was of great help on this project. I'd like to thank my good friends Jay and Carolyn Mirowitz, who were my biggest fans from the start of this book, for their reading of my manuscript and their encouragement along the way. Also a special thanks to Monica and Don Poole, owners of the wonderful bookstore One for the Books in Cape Coral, Florida. Their help was greatly appreciated as was the company of their cat, Aggie. I'd like to thank my husband's daughter, Annie Brennen, who continues to support me in my endeavors, and her mother, Dr. Bonnie Brennen, a cat fancier who gave up her favorite cat book for my research. I'd like to thank my husband's son, J. Scott Brennen, for his hours of computer work, proofing of my manuscript, and the scanning of photographs. A special thanks goes to publisher Nick Lyons whose help, kindness, and advice throughout this project was greatly appreciated.

Thanks to my veterinarian, Kirk S. Andazola of the Coral Veterinary Clinic in Fort Myers, Florida, whose love of cats, and insights into their ills, both physical and psychological, gave me a greater understanding when writing about Hemingway's cats. I want to thank Kathy Beekman, past owner of Sanibel Island's Moto Photo, and her assistant, Tommy Hott, for their excellent service, and Hollie Smith, an animal lover and the proprietor of the marvelous little bookstore Sanibel Island Book Shop on Sanibel Island, Florida, who continues to keep the research books coming. Thanks to Faye Matthews for her computer expertise and support throughout this book project. A special thanks to my brother, Bill Semmer, who has been my staunch supporter throughout this endeavor, and to members of his staff at Semmer Electric on San Carlos Island, Florida, Jan Arding, Sandy Bianchi, and Ayita Rainey, for their help. I'd like to thank my good friend John Richard and my brother Bill Semmer for their assistance while I was in Cuba. Their help on this project was invaluable, and I would never have had the opportunity to collect the last valuable photographs and research material at Finca Vigia's Museo Ernest Hemingway without their assistance. To my sister-in-law, Shirley Semmer, goes a special thanks. She continues to offer her expertise in everything, including her computer skills. And thanks to my goddaughter, Katie Semmer, and to my nephew, Billy Semmer, for their support. Thanks to my dear friend Jeanne Kirschner for her encouragement. Thanks to librarian Pat Allen at the Sanibel Library for her advice. I'd like to thank my niece, Krissy Baker, and Michael Fisher, whose love of animals is becoming legendary, and Tracey and Henry Gore and Pam and Will Yates for their support. I would like to thank manager Barbara Whatley and Margie Titus of Bonita Bill's Waterfront Café on San Carlos Island for their friendship and for the companionship of Barb's cat, Splash. The café's wonderful "pet-friendly" open-air dining room was a great place to write. Thanks to Anne Bellew, Holly Batchelor and Ed Batchelor for their kindness, and also to Nora Price, Jane and Dan Lumley, Gilda and Joe Suarez, and George and Nancy Madison, for their friendship. A special thanks to Willy Becker for remodeling my office when I desperately needed more space. A special thanks to my half-brother Gregory Semmer and his family in Chicago. It was so wonderful to meet you after all these years.

I would like to thank Willow Martell for her kindness in allowing me to use her office to complete this book, as well as the companionship of her beloved pets, Mia and Ben. And a thank-you to Suzanne Boettcher, who is as much of an animal lover as I am, for the gracious use of her home during this project. A special thanks to the wonderful volunteers of P.A.W.S., who have rescued and found homes for hundreds of cats on Sanibel Island, and in memory of Ellen Smith who gave her heart and soul to this worthwhile organization. I would also like to thank Carol Palumbo, Lynda and Ken Boyce, Lou Palumbo, Leroy and Maxine Henderson, Dr. August and Tommy Freudlich, Jake and Mary Hemingway, and Tommie Hemingway Mulder, as well as Craig Albert, Nora Mohr, Tony Gropp, and Mary Griswold at Sanibel-Captiva Community Bank for their support. Thanks to Terri Blackmore, Beryl Gray, and Captain Bill Gartrell, whose kindness and love of animals matches only Hemingway's deep devotion to his pets. A special thanks goes to my sisters, Lorraine Baldwin, Joanne Semmer, and Betty Hill, and my nephew Eli Baldwin, not only for finding homes for the unwanted cats and kittens on San Carlos Island, but for their continued search for books for my ongoing research. I would like to thank my attorney and good friend Michael F. Hornung, who is always there when I need his advice, and to his paralegal, Catherine Battaglia, for her assistance. A special thanks to my C.P.A., Keith M. Silver, who did his best to help me get published, and to his assistants, June Zeller and Ken Bryant, for their friendship and support. Thank you to Gary Price, who loves history as much as I, and to Lee Melsek, the best investigating reporter I know, whose integrity is without reproach. A special thanks to Gene Hamilton, who worked for Hemingway as a yard boy. I can't thank him enough for his memories of his Key West days.

A special thanks to my doctors and good friends, Dr. Steve Zellner and Dr. Allen B. Shevach, for their care during this time. I'd also like to thank Dr. Susanna Beshai, Dr. Lorraine M. Golosow, Dr. Michael P. Gross and his staff, Dr. William Harwin, Dr. Paul Liccini, and his assistant, Teresa Funk, and staff, for their kindness and care. I'd like to thank John Kanzius, whose support has been greatly appreciated, and who I hope finds the funds needed for his marvelous noninvasive cancer treatment with radio waves. The researchers are calling it the Holy Grail cure for cancer. And to dear friend, Dr. Harvey Tritel, a special thanks for his continued friendship. His phone calls kept my spirits up, and his humor was greatly appreciated. And thanks to his son, Dr. Paul Tritel, for his thoughtfulness. I wrote several chapters of this book during my hospital stays recovering from breast cancer surgery, and the work on this book proved better than any pain medicine or sedative I could have taken.

I would like to thank literary agent Peter Rubie, a cat lover and owner of cats, for his encouragement and kindness.

A special thank you to Bugsy, Princess of the Wild, Charlie, Little Kitty, Murphy, Max, and Teddy for giving me unconditional love and "valuable aid." And to Chipsy, Mitzi, Keytai, Kugel, Snow Lamb, and Nikki—for fond memories—and to Edgar, Walter, Wiskers, Mel, Panther, Smokey, and Henry, who have brightened up my life.

In memory of Bugsy and Murphy, whom I dearly miss every day.

Bibliography

Andrew, David, and Susan Rind. *Watching Wildlife: East Africa.* Melbourne: Lonely Planet Publications, 2001.

Arnold, Lloyd. *Hemingway High on the Wild.* New York: Grosset & Dunlap Publishers, 1968.

Arnold, Tillie. *The Idaho Hemingway.* Buhl, Idaho: Beacon Books, 1999.

Bach, Steven. *Marlene Dietrich: Life and Legend.* New York: Da Capo Press. W. Marrow, 1992.

Baker, Carlos. *Ernest Hemingway: A Life Story.* New York: Charles Scribner's Sons, 1969.

Baker, Carlos. *Hemingway: The Writer as Artist.* Princeton, New Jersey: Princeton University Press, 1963.

Becker, Dr. Marty, with Danelle Morton. *The Healing Power of Pets.* New York: Hyperion, 2002.

Beegel, Susan F., ed. *Hemingway's Neglected Short Fiction: New Perspectives.* Tuscaloosa, Alabama: University of Alabama Press, 1989.

Benson, Jackson J., ed., *The Short Stories of Ernest Hemingway: Critical Essays.* Durham, North Carolina: Duke University Press, 1975.

Berg, A. Scott. *Max Perkins: Editor of Genius.* New York: E.P. Dutton, 1978.

Boreth, Craig. *The Hemingway Cookbook.* Chicago: Chicago Review Press, 1998.

Brian, Denis. *The True Gen: An Intimate Portrait of Hemingway by Those Who Knew Him.* New York: Grove Press, 1988.

Bruccoli, Matthew J., ed. *Conversations with Ernest Hemingway.* Jackson, Mississippi: University Press of Mississippi, 1986.

Bruccoli, Matthew J., ed. *The Only Thing That Counts.* New York: Scribner's, 1996.

Bryant, Doris. *The Care and Handling of CATS: A Manual For Modern Cat Owners.* New York: Ives Washburn, Inc., 1944.

Burgess, Anthony. *Ernest Hemingway and His World.* New York: Charles Scribner's Sons, 1985.

Burrill, William. *Hemingway: The Toronto Years.* Toronto: Doubleday Canada Limited, 1994.

Caras, Roger A. *A Celebration of Cats.* New York: Simon & Schuster. 1986.

Carr, William H. A. *The Basic Book of the Cat.* New York: Gramercy Publishing Company. n.d.

Chittock, Lorraine. *Cats of Cairo: Egypt's Enduring Legacy.* New York: Abbeville Press, 2000.

Conrad, Barnaby. Photographs by Loomis Dean. *Hemingway's Spain.* San Francisco: Chronicle Books, 1989.

Conrad, Winston. *Hemingway's France: Images of the Lost Generation.* Emeryville, California: Woodford Press, 2000.

Conway, D. J. *The Mysterious, Magical Cat: A Complete Look at the Wonder of Claw and*

Whisker. New York: Gramercy Books, 1998.

Cowley, Malcolm. *The Dream of the Golden Mountains*. New York: Viking Press, 1980.

Cunliffe, Juliette. *The Encyclopedia of Dog Breeds*. Bath, U.K.: Parragon Publishing, 1999.

Cutts, Paddy. *The Complete Cat Book*. London: Hermes House, an Imprint of Ames Publishing, 1996, update 2001.

de Cortanze, Gérard. Photographs by Jean-Bernard Naudin. *Hemingway in Cuba*. Paris: Editions du Chêne, 1997.

DeFazio III, Albert J., ed. *Dear Papa, Dear Hotch: The Correspondence of Ernest Hemingway and A. E. Hotchner*. Columbia, Missouri: University of Missouri Press, 2005.

Dietrich, Marlene. *Marlene*. New York: Grove Press, 1987.

Diliberto, Gioia. *Hadley*. New York: Ticknor & Fields, 1992.

Donaldson, Scott. *Archibald Macleish: An American Life*. Boston: Houghton Mifflin Company, 1992.

Donaldson, Scott, ed. *The Cambridge Companion to Ernest Hemingway*. Cambridge: Cambridge University Press, 1996.

Donaldson, Scott. *Hemingway vs. Fitzgerald: The Rise and Fall of a Literary Friendship*. New York: The Overlook Press, 1999.

Donnelly, Honoria Murphy, with Richard N Billings. *Sara and Gerald: Villa America and After*. New York: Holt, Rinehart and Winston, 1982.

Duncan, Dayton, Ken Burns, and Geoffrey C. Ward. *Mark Twain: An Illustrated Biography*. New York: Alfred A. Knopf, 2001.

Elliot, Charles, ed. *The Greatest Cat Stories Ever Told*. Guilford, Connecticut: Lyons Press, 2001.

Farrington, S. Kip. Jr. *Fishing with Hemingway and Glassell*. New York: David McKay Company, 1971.

Fitch, Noel Riley. *Sylvia Beach and the Lost Generation: A History of Literary Paris in the Twenties and Thirties*. New York: W.W. Norton & Company, 1993.

Foss, Clive. *Fidel Castro*. Stroud, U. K.: Sutton Publishing, 2000.

Franklin, Jane. *Cuba and the United States: A Chronological History*. New York: Ocean Press, 1997.

Fuentes, Norberto. *Ernest Hemingway Rediscovered*. New York: Charles Scribner's Sons, 1988.

Fuentes, Norberto. *Hemingway in Cuba*. Secaucus, New Jersey: Lyle Stuart, 1984.

Gardner, Carol Hemingway. Morris Buske, ed. "Recollections." *The Hemingway Review* 24.1 (Fall 2004): 17–18.

Gellhorn, Martha. *Travels with Myself and Another*. London: Allen Lane, 1978; New York: Jeremy P. Tarcher/Putnam, 2001.

Gerogiannis, Nicholas, ed. *Ernest Hemingway Complete Poems*. Lincoln, Nebraska: University of Nebraska Press, 1979, 1983, 1992.

Gerstenfeld, Sheldon L. *Taking Care of Your Cat: A Complete Guide to Your Cat's Medical Care*. Reading, Massachusetts: Addison-Wesley, 1979.

Griffin, Peter. *Less Than a Treason: Hemingway in Paris*. New York: Oxford University Press, 1990.

Hausman, Gerald, and Loretta Hausman. *The Mythology of Cats.* New York: Berkley Books, 1998.

Hemingway, Carol. "907 Whitehead Street." *The Hemingway Review* 23.1 (Fall 2003): 8–23.

Hemingway, Gregory H. *Papa: A Personal Memoir.* Boston: Houghton Mifflin, 1976.

Hemingway, Hilary. "The Hemingways and Diabetes." *International Hemingway Festival Book 3* 1999: 14–15.

Hemingway, Hilary, and Carlene F. Brennen. *Hemingway in Cuba.* New York: Rugged Land, 2003.

Hemingway, Jack. *A Life Worth Living: The Adventures of a Passionate Sportsman.* Guilford, Connecticut: Lyons Press, 2002.

Hemingway, Jack. *Misadventures of a Fly Fisherman: My Life With and Without Papa.* Dallas, Texas: Taylor Publishing Company (a division of the Rowman and Littlefield Publishing Group, Lanham, MD), 1986.

Hemingway, Patricia Shedd. *Grow Old Along With Me.* (Edited and published for personal family enjoyment by Mary and Jake Hemingway), n.d.

Hemingway, Leicester. *My Brother, Ernest Hemingway.* New York: World Publishing, 1961; Sarasota, Florida: Pineapple Press, 1996.

Hemingway, Mary Welsh. *How It Was.* New York: Alfred Knopf, 1976.

Hemingway, Valerie. "*The Garden of Eden* Revisited: With Hemingway in Provence in the Summer of '59." *The Hemingway Review* 18.2 (Centennial Issue 1999): 102–113.

Hemingway, Valerie. *Running with the Bulls: My Years with the Hemingways.* New York: Ballantine Books, 2004.

Horton-Bussey, Claire, and David Godfrey. *Cat Owner's Survival Manual.* Dorking, Surrey, U.K.: Ring Press Books, 2002.

Hotchner, A. E. *Hemingway and His World.* London: Viking Press, 1999.

Hotchner, A. E. "Papa Hemingway," *The Saturday Evening Post,* March 12, 1961.

Hotchner, A. E. *Papa Hemingway: A Personal Memoir.* New York: Random House, 1966; New York: Carroll & Graf, 1999. Cambridge, Massachusetts: Da Capo Press, 2005.

Kert, Bernice. *The Hemingway Women.* New York: W.W. Norton and Company, 1983.

Kert, Bernice. "Jane Mason and Ernest Hemingway: A Biographer Reviews Her Notes." *The Hemingway Review* 21.2 (Safari Special Issue 2002): 111–116.

Kreuz, Tamara. *The Stray Cat Handbook.* New York: Howell Book House, 1999.

Lane, Marion S. *The Humane Society of the United States Complete Guide to Dog Care.* Boston: Little, Brown and Company, 1998.

Lania, Leo. *Hemingway: A Pictorial Biography.* New York: The Viking Press, 1961.

Loxton, Howard. *99 Lives: Cats in History, Legend and Literature.* New York: Barnes & Noble Books, 2002.

Lynn, Kenneth S. *Hemingway.* Cambridge, Massachusetts: Harvard University Press, 1987.

MacLeish, Archibald. "His Mirror Was Danger," *Life* magazine, July 14, 1961.

Marth, Marty. *Florida Cat Owner's Handbook.* Sarasota, Florida: Pineapple Press, 1993.

Maziarka, Cynthia, and Donald Vogel Jr., eds. *Hemingway at Oak Park High: The High*

School Writings of Ernest Hemingway, 1916–1917. Oak Park, Illinois: Oak Park and River Forest High School, 1993.

McIver, Stuart B. *Hemingway's Key West*. Sarasota, Florida: Pineapple Press, 2002.

McLendon, James. *Papa: Hemingway in Key West*. Key West, Florida: Langley Press, 1990.

Mellow, James R. *Hemingway: A Life without Consequences*. New York: Houghton Mifflin Company, 1992.

Méry, Fernand. *The Life, History and Magic of the Cat*. New York: Grosset and Dunlap Publishers, 1968.

Metcalf, Christine. *Cats: History, Care, Breeds*. New York.: Grosset and Dunlap. 1970.

Meyers, Jeffrey. *Bogart: A Life in Hollywood*. Boston: Houghton Mifflin Company, 1997.

Meyers, Jeffrey. *Hemingway: A Biography*. New York: Harper and Row Publishers, 1985.

Meyers, Jeffrey, ed. *Hemingway: The Critical Heritage*. London: Routledge and Kegan Paul, 1983.

Miller, Linda Patterson, ed. *Letters from the Lost Generation*. Gainesville, Florida: University Press of Florida, 2002

Miller, Madelaine Hemingway. *Ernie: Hemingway's Sister "Sunny" Remembers*. New York: Crown Publishers, 1975.

Moorehead, Caroline. *Gellhorn: A Twentieth-Century Life*. New York: Henry Holt and Company, 2003.

Morris, Desmond. *Cat World: A Feline Encyclopedia*. New York: Penguin Books USA, 1997.

Nemec, Gale B. *Living with Cats*. New York: William Morrow, 1993.

Oliver, Charles M. *Ernest Hemingway A to Z: The Essential Reference to the Life and Work*. New York: Facts on File, 1999.

Ondaatje, Christopher. *Hemingway in Africa: The Last Safari*. New York: Overlook Press, 2004.

O'Shea, Mark, and Tim Halliday. S*mithsonian's Handbooks: Reptiles and Amphibians*. London: Dorling Kindersley, 2001.

Page, Tim, ed. *The Diaries of Dawn Powell 1931–1965*. South Royalton, Vermont: Steerforth Press, 1965.

Palin, Michael. *Michael Palin's Hemingway Adventure*. New York: St. Martins Press, 1999.

Paul, Steve. "On Hemingway and His Influence: Conversations With Writers." *The Hemingway Review* 18.2 (Centennial Issue 1999): 115–132.

Paul, Steve. "Preparing for War and Writing: What the Young Hemingway Read in *The Kansas City Star, 1917–1918.*" *The Hemingway Review* 23.2 (Spring 2004): 5–20.

Percival, Phillip H. *Hunting, Settling and Remembering*. Agoura, California: Trophy Room Books, 1997.

Plimpton, George A. "Ernest Hemingway: The Art of Fiction XXI." *The Paris Review* 18 (Fifth Anniversary Issue, Spring 1958): 61–89.

Plath, James, and Frank Simmons. *Remembering Ernest Hemingway*. Key West, Florida: Ketch and Yawl Press, 1999.

Pollard, Michael. *The Encyclopedia of the Cat*. London: Parragon Publishing. 1999.

Reiger, George. "The Literary Naturalist" in *Profiles in Saltwater Angling*. Englewood Cliffs, New Jersey: Prentice Hall, 1973.

Reynolds, Michael. *Hemingway: The 1930s*. New York: W.W. Norton, 1997.

Reynolds, Michael. *Hemingway: The American Homecoming*. New York: W.W. Norton, 1992.

Reynolds, Michael. *Hemingway: The Final Years*. New York: W.W. Norton, 1999.

Reynolds, Michael. *Hemingway: The Paris Years*. New York: W.W. Norton, 1989.

Reynolds, Michael. *Hemingway's First War: The Making of* A Farewell to Arms. Princeton, New Jersey: Princeton University Press, 1976; New York: Basil Blackwell, 1987.

Reynolds, Michael. *The Young Hemingway*. New York: Basil Blackwell, 1986.

Richards, James R. *ASPCA® Complete Guide to Cats*. San Francisco: Chronicle Books, 1999.

Richards, Norman. *People of Destiny: Ernest Hemingway*. Chicago: Children's Press, 1968.

Riva, Maria. *Marlene Dietrich*. New York: Alfred A. Knopf, 1993.

Rollyson, Carl. *Beautiful Exile: The Life of Martha Gellhorn*. London: Aureen Press, 2002.

Rollyson, Carl. *Nothing Ever Happens to the Brave: The Story of Martha Gellhorn*. New York: St. Martin's Press, 1990.

Ross, Lillian. *Portrait of Hemingway*. New York: The Modern Library/Random House, 1999.

Sandison, David. *Ernest Hemingway: An Illustrated Biography*. Chicago: Chicago Review Press, 1999.

Sanford, Marcelline Hemingway. *At the Hemingways: A Family Portrait*. Boston: Little, Brown, 1962; Centennial Edition. With Fifty Years of Correspondence Between Ernest and Marcelline Hemingway, edited by John Sanford. Moscow, Idaho: University of Idaho Press, 1999.

Schleden, Ina Mae, and Marion Rawls Herzog. *Ernest Hemingway as Recalled by His High School Contemporaries*. Oak Park, Illinois: The Historical Society of Oak Park and River Forest, 1973.

Scribner Jr., Charles. *In the Company of Writers: A Life in Publishing*. New York: Charles Scribner's Sons, 1990.

Seals, Marc. "Reclaimed Experience: Trauma Theory And Hemingway's Lost Paris Manuscripts." *The Hemingway Review* 24.2 (Spring 2005): 62–72.

Sinclair, Gail. "An Interview With Papa's Little Sister." *The Hemingway Review* 24.1 (Fall 2004) 8–16.

Sinclair, Gail. "Carol and Ernest Hemingway: The Letters of Loss." *The Hemingway Review* 24.1 (Fall 2004) 37–48.

Stanton, Edward F. *Hemingway and Spain: A Pursuit*. Seattle: University of Washington Press, 1989.

Shnayerson, Michael. *Irwin Shaw: A Biography*. New York: G.P. Putnam's Sons, 1989.

Sokoloff, Alice Hunt. *Hadley: The First Mrs. Hemingway*. New York: Dodd, Mead and Company, 1973.

Stein, Gertrude. *The Autobiography of Alice B. Toklas*. New York: The Modern Library,

1993; New York. Harcourt, Brace and Company, 1933.

Stendahl, Renate, ed. *Gertrude Stein in Words and Pictures: A Photobiography.* Chapel Hill, North Carolina: Algonquin Books, 1994.

Svoboda, Frederic J., and Joseph J. Waldmeir, eds. *Hemingway: Up in Michigan Perspectives.* East Lansing, Michigan: Michigan State University Press, 1995.

Szulc, Tad. *Fidel: A Critical Portrait.* New York: Avon Books, 1986.

Thomas, Hugh. *Cuba: The Pursuit of Freedom.* New York: Harper and Row, 1971.

Trogdon, Robert W., ed. *Ernest Hemingway: A Literary Reference.* New York: Carroll and Graff, 1999.

Turnbull, Andrew, ed. *The Letters of F. Scott Fitzgerald.* New York: Charles Scribner's Sons. 1963.

Turnbull, Andrew. *Scott Fitzgerald.* New York: Grove Press, 1962.

Vaill, Amanda. *Everybody Was So Young: Gerald and Sara Murphy: A Lost Generation Love Story.* New York: Broadway Books, 1999.

Villard, Henry S., and James Nagel. *Hemingway in Love and War: The Lost Diary of Agnes Von Kurowsky.* Boston: Northeastern University Press, 1989.

Voss, Frederick. *Picturing Hemingway: A Writer in His Times.* New Haven: Yale University Press, 1999.

Wagner-Martin, Linda, ed. *A Historical Guide to Ernest Hemingway.* New York: Oxford University Press, 2000.

Wheelock, John Hall, ed. *Editor to Author: The Letters of Maxwell E. Perkins.* Atlanta, Georgia: Cherokee Publishing Company, 1991.

Whiting, Charles. *Papa Goes to War: Ernest Hemingway in Europe, 1944–45.* Marlborough, U.K.: Crowood Press, 1990.

Williams, J.G. *A Field Guide to the National Parks of East Africa.* London: William Collin's Sons and Co. Ltd., 1967.

Young, Philip. *Ernest Hemingway: A Reconsideration.* University Park: Pennsylvania State University Press, 1966.

By Ernest Hemingway

Three Stories & Ten Poems. Paris: Contract Publishing, 1923.

In Our Time. Paris: Three Mountain Press, 1925; and New York: Charles Scribner's Sons, 1925.

The Torrents of Spring. New York: Charles Scribner's Sons, 1926.

The Sun Also Rises. New York: Charles Scribner's Sons, 1926.

Men Without Women. New York: Charles Scribner's Sons, 1927.

A Farewell to Arms. New York: Charles Scribner's Sons, 1929.

Death in the Afternoon. New York: Charles Scribner's Sons, 1932.

Winner Take Nothing. New York: Charles Scribner's Sons, 1933.

Green Hills of Africa. New York: Charles Scribner's Sons, 1935.

To Have and Have Not. New York: Charles Scribner's Sons, 1937.

For Whom the Bell Tolls. New York: Charles Scribner's Sons, 1940.

"Introduction" and editor, *Men at War: The Best War Stories of All Time.* New York: Crown Publishing, 1942; New York: Wing Books, 1991.

Across the River and into the Trees. New York: Charles Scribner's Sons, 1950.

The Old Man and the Sea. New York: Charles Scribner's Sons, 1952.

"The Christmas Gift." *Look,* April 20 and 27, 1954.

"Visit with Hemingway." *Look,* September 4, 1956.

The Dangerous Summer. New York: Simon & Schuster, 1960.

A Moveable Feast. New York: Charles Scribner's Sons, 1964.

The Fifth Column and Four Stories of the Spanish Civil War. New York: Simon and Schuster, 1969 (First Scribner Paperback Edition, 1998).

Islands in the Stream. New York: Charles Scribner's Sons, 1970.

The Nick Adams Stories. New York: Charles Scribner's Sons, 1972.

Baker, Carlos, ed. *Ernest Hemingway: Selected Letters 1917–1961.* New York: Charles Scribner's Sons, 1981.

Phillips, Larry W., ed. *Ernest Hemingway on Writing.* New York: Charles Scribner's Sons, 1984.

White, William, ed. *Dateline, Toronto: Hemingway's Complete Dispatches for the Toronto Star, 1920–1924.* New York. Charles Scribners' Sons, 1985.

The Garden of Eden. New York: Charles Scribner's Sons, 1986.

The Complete Short Stories of Ernest Hemingway: The Finca Vigia Edition. New York: Charles Scribner's Sons, 1987.

White, William, ed. *By-Line Ernest Hemingway: Selected Articles and Dispatches of Four Decades.* New York: Simon & Schuster, 1967, 1995; first Touchstone edition, 1998.

Hemingway, Patrick, ed. *True at First Light.* New York: Scribner's, 1999.

Lyons, Nick, ed. *Hemingway on Fishing.* New York: Lyons Press, 2000.

Hemingway, Sean, ed. *Hemingway on Hunting.* Guilford, Connecticut: Lyons Press, 2001.

Hemingway, Sean, ed. *Hemingway on War.* New York: Charles Scribner's Sons, 2003.

Author's Note

Ernest Hemingway told his editor Max Perkins in 1933 that he had plans to write his "Ultimate Memoirs" because of his "rat-trap memory." His books *A Moveable Feast, Islands in the Stream, The Garden of Eden,* and *True at First Light,* according to family and close friends, were as close as Hemingway ever came to writing his autobiography. After his death in 1961 all of these books were eventually published. But what makes these works so important to Hemingway's legacy is that they were all written late in the author's life when most of us begin to reflect about our past while still dealing with the present. These works offered me a rare insight into one of the nation's most loved and important writers.—*Carlene Fredericka Brennen*

Photo Credits

The Ernest Hemingway Collection
John F. Kennedy Presidential Library and Museum, Boston
ii, iii, v, vi, viii, ix *top*, ix *bottom*, x, xiv, 1 *top*, 1 *bottom*, 2 *top*, 2 *bottom*, 3, 4, 5 *top*, 7, 8, 9 *top*, 9 *bottom*, 11, 12, 13 *top*, 14, 16, 18, 20, 21 *bottom*, 23 *top*, 23 *bottom*, 25, 27 *top*, 34, 35 *bottom*, 39, 40 *top*, 40 *bottom*, 44 *top*, 46, 48, 49, 50, 51, 52, 53, 54, 55 *top*, 56, 61, 62, 65 *top*, 66 *bottom*, 68, 69 *top*, 69 *bottom*, 70, 71, 75, 76, 78, 80, 81, 82, 84, 87, 88, 89 *top*, 91, 93, 94, 95, 96, 97, 99, 100, 101, 106, 110, 111, 114, 116, 117, 118, 119, 120, 122, 123, 125, 128, 129, 131, 132, 133, 141 *bottom*, 142, 143, 146, 148, 149, 150, 151, 152, 154, 155, 163, 166, 174

Carlene Fredericka Brennen
vii, xiii, 5 *middle*, 5 *bottom*, 6 *top*, 6 *bottom*, 10, 13 *bottom*, 15, 19 *top*, 19 *bottom*, 21 *top*, 27 *bottom*, 28 *top*, 28 *bottom*, 30 *bottom*, 31 *top*, 31 *bottom*, 33 *top*, 33 *bottom*, 36 *top*, 36 *bottom*, 38, 41, 43 *left*, 44 *bottom*, 45, 47, 55 *bottom*, 57, 58 *top*, 58 *bottom*, 59, 60, 65 *bottom*, 72, 83 *top*, 83 *middle*, 86 *top*, 86 *middle*, 89 *bottom*, 92, 102, 103, 104, 105, 107, 108 *top*, 108 *bottom*, 109, 112 *top*, 130, 134, 136, 140, 144, 147 *top*, 147 *bottom*, 161, 162 *left*, 162 *right*, 164

The Estate of Leicester Hemingway
xi, 13 *middle*, 22, 26, 32, 64, 66 top, 74, 83 *bottom*, 98, 135, 158

Hans Malmburg, Tiofoto
85, 90, 124, 126, 137, 138, 145

Museo Ernest Hemingway, Cuba
86 *bottom*, 112 *bottom*

Getty Images, 17
Florida State Archives, 30 *top*, 35 *top*, 37
The Estate of Sara Murphy, 156
Bob Swinker, xiii
Debby Getch, 43 *right*

Permissions

On page 27:
From *The Torrents of Spring* by Ernest Hemingway, reprinted with permission of Scribner, an imprint of Simon & Schuster Adult Publishing group. Copyright 1926 by Charles Scribner's Sons. Copyright renewed 1954 by Ernest Hemingway.

On pages 117, 119, 120, 121:
From *True at First Light* by Ernest Hemingway, reprinted with permission of Scribner, an imprint of Simon & Schuster Adult Publishing group. Copyright © 1999.

On pages 73, 74, 81, 83, 117, 120, 140, 143, 161, 162:
From *How It Was* by Mary Welsh Hemingway, copyright © 1951, 1955, 1963, 1966, 1976 by Mary Welsh Hemingway. Used by permission of Alfred A. Knopf, a division of Random House, Inc.

On page 10:
Excerpt from *Hemingway: A Life without Consequences* by James R. Mellow. Copyright © 1992 by James R. Mellow. Reprints by permission of Houghton Mifflin Company. All rights reserved.

On page 42:
Excerpt from April 1939 letter. Printed with the permission of The Ernest Hemingway Foundation.

On page 42:
Excerpt from 1949 letter. Printed with the permission of The Ernest Hemingway Foundation.

On page 72:
Excerpt from 1946 letter. Printed with the permission of The Ernest Hemingway Foundation.

On page 79:
Excerpt from May 1945 letter. Printed with the permission of The Ernest Hemingway Foundation.

On page 86, 87:
Excerpt from September 1945 letter. Printed with the permission of The Ernest Hemingway Foundation.

On page 140, 142:
Excerpt from 1960 letter. Printed with the permission of The Ernest Hemingway Foundation.

On page 9, 11:
From *Hemingway in Love and War: The Lost Diary of Agnes von Kurowsky* by Henry S. Villard and James Nagel. Copyright © 1989 University Press of New England, Hanover, NH. Reprinted with permission.

On page 66:
From *At the Hemingways: A Family Portrait* by Marcelline Hemingway Sanford. Copyright (c) 1998 by John E. Sanford. Reprinted by permission of John E. Sanford. All rights reserved.

On page 42:
From *Everybody Was So Young: Gerald and Sara Murphy, A Lost Generation Love Story* by Amanda Vaill. Copyright (c) 1998 by Amanda Vaill Stewart. Reprinted by permission of Houghton Mifflin Company. All rights reserved.

Index

A

Across the River and into the Trees, 113
Africa, SS, 122
Aigues-Mortes, France, 24
Allen, Didi, 92
Ambos Mundos Hotel, Havana, 45, 178
Ambrose Bierce (*see* cats in Cuba)
Ambrosio (*see* cats in Cuba)
American Red Cross Hospital, 9, 10
Anderson, Sherwood, 15
Arguelles, Elian, 128
Arnold, Lloyd "Pappy," 92
Arnold, Tillie, 155, 157
Ashley, Lady Brett, 24

B

Baa (baby Grant's gazelle), 117
Baby (*see* cats in Cuba)
Bach, Steven, 74, 139
Baker, Carlos, 42, 45, 69, 70, 71, 73, 111,
   113, 123, 136, 137, 147, 148, 149,
   153, 160, 172, 181
Barbershop (*see* cats in Cuba)
Barclay Hotel, New York, 45
Barkley, Catherine, 28
Barnes, Jake, 24
Bates (*see* cats in Cuba)
Batista, Fulgencio, 57, 115, 135, 136, 137,
   159–160, 161, 172, 173
Batista, Panchin, 144
Bay of Pigs invasion, 153
Beach, Sylvia, 20
Beaulac, Willard, 160
Becker, Dr. Marty, 2, 3, 6, 45, 47, 153,
   181
Big Boy Peterson (*see* cats in Idaho and out
   West)
Big Goats (*see* cats in Cuba)

Big Wood River, Idaho, 141, 142
Bigotes (*see* cats in Cuba)
Bird, William "Bill," 20
Black Dog (*see* dogs in Cuba)
black mamba (*see* snakes)
Blackie (*see* dogs in Cuba)
Blindie (*see* cats in Cuba)
Bogart, Humphrey, 127
Boise (*see* cats in Cuba)
Boissy D'Angelas (*see* cats in Cuba)
Bourne, Catherine, 91
Bourne, David, 67, 118, 119
Boy (*see* cats in Cuba)
Boysy (*see* cats in Cuba)
Bradfield, Ruth, 13
Bradley, Helen, 41
Breaker, Helen, 13
Breit, Harvey, 123
Brian, Denis, 74
Briggs, Ellis, 70
Bro (*see* cats in Cuba)
Browning, Elizabeth Barrett, 113, 144,
   148, 149
Bruce, Toby, 35
Bryant, Doris, 86, 97
Bryn Mawr, 39
Bullfights, 29, 147, 148
Bumby (*see* Hemingway, John Hadley
   Nicanor "Bumby")
Burrell, Mark, 33
Butiaba, Uganda, 121
Butt, Dr. Hugh R., 151
By-Line Ernest Hemingway, 99, 100, 187

C

Cannell, Kitty, 21, 24,
Carr, William H.A., 157, 181
Cartwright, Reggie, 121

Casper, Wyoming, 91
Castro, Fidel, 57, **158**, 159, 161, **161**, 178
cat cemetery at Finca Vigia, 109, 131, 165, 171
Cat in the Rain, 15, 16
Cathedral of the Sacred Heart (Sacré Coeur), 17
Catherine the Great, 6
Catherine Tiger (*see* cats in Oak Park)
Catholic Church, 155
cats
    in Africa, 120
    in Cuba,
        abandoned cats, 57, 101
        Ambrose (Ambrose Bierce, Ambrosio), 165
        Angora tiger cats, 49
        Bates, 63, 165, 169
        Blindie, 71, 72, 75, 165
        boat cats, 66
        Boise (Dillinger, Dingie, Boy, Boysy, Boissy D'Angelas), **ii**, **v**, 33, 48, **48**, 49, **49**, 50, **50**, 51, **51**, **52**, **53**, **54**, 55, **55**, **56**, 63, 65, **65**, 68, 70, 71, **80**, 82, 83, **83**, **84**, **85**, 87, **90**, 92, 95, 96, 102, 107, 109, 113, 115, 120, **123**, 125, **126**, 127, 128, **128**, 129, **130**, 131, **131**, 133, 135, 139, 147, 155, 163, 165, 166, 167, 168, 169, 170, 171
        and catnip, 48, 49, 63, 65, 81, 83, 86, 102, 168
        and circus tricks, 65, **65**, 168, 171
        in Cojimar, 52, 53, 72, 131, 165
        cotsies, 63, 75, 86, 87, 174
        Crazy Christian, 166, **166**
        Cristóbal (Christopher Columbus, Cristóbal Colón, Stobbs), **vi**, **132**, 133, 140, 143, **150**, 151, **151**, 153, **154**, 155, 160, 161, 166, 167, 168
        Ecstasy (Smelly), 81, **93**, 107, 109, 167, 170
        Fatso (Fats), 55, 71, 81, 95, **95**, 97,

97, 109, 167
        Feather Kitty, 20, 23, 25, 133, 166, 167, 168
        Finca cats, **43**, 44, 45, 46, 47, 48, 49, 50, 53, 55, 60, 65, 70, 71, 72, 81, **81**, 82, **82**, 83, **87**, **88**, **93**, 95, 101, 107, 108, 109, 124, 129, 131, 133, 136, 140, 145, 147, 153, 160
        Friendless (Bigotes, Big Goats, Goats), 55, 63, 69, **69**, 70, 71, 72, 81, 87, **94**, 95, **95**, 96, **96**, 97, **97**, 102, **106**, 109, 166, 167, 168
        Friendless' Brother (Bro), 55, 72, 76, **76**, 81, 86, **86**, **97**, 102, 107, **110**, 127, 167, 168, 170
        Furhouse, 55, 63, 72, 81, 167, 168, 170
        Good Will (Will), **v**, 48, **48**, 50, 51, 55, **55**, 65, 71, 72, 76, 81, 102, 168
        Izzy the Cat (Izzy, Isabella la Católica, the queen), **132**, 133, 166, 168
        Littless Kitty (Nuisance Value), **64**, 72, 81, 169
        Pelusa, 147, 169
        Pony, 63, 165, 169
        Princessa (Tester, Baby), **v**, 46, 47, 48, **48**, 49, 51, 55, 62, 65, 71, 79, 81, 87, **87**, 96, 102, 107, 163, 165, 166, 167, 168, 169, 170, 171
        Shopsky (Shakespeare, Barbershop), 81, **93**, 109, 167, 170
        Sir Winston Churchill, 170
        Spendy (Stephen Spender, Spendthrift), 81, **93**, 102, 109, 167, 170
        Stranger, 170
        stray cats, 44, 45, 47, 49, 50, 57, 71, **71**, **107**, **164**, 178
        Taskforce, 170
        Thruster (Thrusty), **43**, 44, 55, 63, 71, 72, 73, 81, 82, 83, 133, 165, 167, 168, 170
        Uncle Wolfer (Wolfer, Uncle Wolfie,

Stoopy, Stoopy Wolfer, Snow
    Leopard), **46**, 63, 65, 72, 81, 102,
    171
Willy (Willie, Mr. Willy, Uncle
    Willy), 48, 49, 50, 51, 63, 76, **76**,
    81, **93**, 102, 107, 109, 113, 129,
    130, 166, 167, 171
in Egypt, 47
in Idaho and out West,
    Big Boy Peterson, 140, 142, **142**, 143,
        147, 149, **149**, **151**, 153, 155,
        165
    Miss Kitty, 91, 92, 169
    Mooky, 65, 169
    Sister Kitty, 140, 143, 165, 170
    wild cats, 92, **92**
in Italy,
    rescued kitten, 10
in Key West, 27, 28, 31, **33**, 35, 36,
        38, 47
    café cats, 28, **38**
    feral cats, 27, **27**
    Hemingway cats, 33, 39
    neighborhood cats, 31, **31**, 33, 34,
        34, 35, **35**, 36, **43**
    painted cat, 36, **37**
    polydactyl cats, 28, **28**, 31, **31**, 33,
        36, **36**
    Snowball, 36, 170
in New York,
    Dawn Powell's cat, 73
in Oak Park, **5**, **6**
    Catherine Tiger, 5, 6
    family cats, 1, 5, 6
    Manx, 1, 169
in Paris, 15, 16, 17, 21, **21**
    F. Puss (Feather Puss), 19, 21, 24, 27,
        47, 64, 167
in Toronto,
    Feather Kcat, 19, 167
in Upper Michigan,
    pet graveyard, 6
    at Walloon Lake, 4, 5
    at Windermere Cottage, 5, 7
in Utah, 92

cats' tower at Finca Vigia, 81, 86, 89, 101,
    102, **103**, **104**, 107, 113, 131, 135,
    162
Central Intelligence Agency, 74
Charles Scribner's Sons, 24
Cheyenne, Wyoming, 45
Chicago Daily News, 24
Chicago, Illinois, 27, 66
Chickie (*see* dogs in Cuba)
Christmas Story, The, 99
Christopher Columbus (*see* cats in Cuba)
circus animals, 66
Cojimar, Cuba, 49, 50, 53, 59, 60, 72, 131
Colliers magazine, 42, 71
Congo River Basin, 121
Constitution, SS, 144,
Contract Publishing, 16
Cooperative Commonwealth, 13
Cotsies Pride (milk cow in Cuba), 174
Cottorro, Cuba, 137
Cowley, Malcolm, 39, 182
Crane, Stephen, 5
Crazy Christian (*see* cats in Cuba)
Cristóbal (*see* cats in Cuba)
Cristóbal Colón (*see* cats in Cuba)
Crook Factory, 69
Crown Publishing, 69
Cuban mongrels (*see* dogs in Cuba)
Cunliffe, Juliette, 136

D
Danby-Smith, Valerie (*see* Hemingway,
    Valerie)
Dangerous Summer, The, 147, 187
Davis, Bill, 144
de Jouvenel, Bertrand, 41
Death in the Afternoon, 1, 9, 144
Debba, Queen of the Ngomas (African
    girl), 120
Dietrich, Marlene, 74, **74**, 111, 139, 155
Diliberto, Gioia, 181
Dillinger (*see* cats in Cuba)
Dingie (*see* cats in Cuba)
dogs
    in Africa,

Kibo, 117, 119, 136, 172
in Austria,
 Schnauz, 100, **100**, 173
in Cuba,
 abandoned dogs, 57, **58**, **59**, 86, 87, 100, 101, 117
 Black Dog (Blackie), **ix**, **x**, 34, 35, 48, 59, **98**, 99, **99**, 100, 101, **101**, 102, 107, 108, 111, 113, 115, 117, **117**, 120, 123, 125, 127, 128, 131, 133, **134**, 135, **135**, 136, **136**, 137, **137**, 139, 147, 162
 Chickie, 172
 Cuban mongrels, **57**, 59, 72, 102, 163
 dogs' graveyard at Finca Vigia, 125, 129, 130, 131, **134**, **136**
 Finca dogs, 56, 60, 61, 81, 83, 98, 99, 102, 108, 112, 113, 114, 115, 117, 125, 127, 133, 134, 135, 136, 137, 138, 144, 145, 153, 162, 163
 Lem, 72, 172
 Machakos, 136, 137, 173
 Negrita, **56**, 57, 59, 60, 81, 83, **83**, 102, 113, 114, 115, 117, 125, 135, 136, **136**, 162, 172, 173
 stray dogs, 57, 58, 59, 60, **108**
 Waterfront dogs, 62
 village dogs, 59, **60**
in Hollywood,
 Lassie, 114
 Rin Tin Tin, 114
in Oak Park,
 Tassel, 2
in Paris,
 Wax Puppy, 16, 19, **19**, 20, 62, 67, 72, 173
Dôme café, Paris, 15
Donnelly, Honoria Murphy, 156
Dorchester Hotel, London, 74
Dos Passos, Katy Smith, 13, 107

E

Ecstasy (*see* cats in Cuba)
Edgar, Carl, 13
Egyptians, ancient, 47
Entebbe, Uganda, 121
Ernest Hemingway: Selected Letters 1917– 1961, 13, 23, 33, 39, 47, 125, 127, 147, 165, 187
Ernst, Connie, 74

F

F.B.I., 153
F. Puss (*see* cats in Paris)
Farewell to Arms, A, 11, 27–29, 185
Farrington, S. Kip, 95
Fats (*see* cats in Cuba)
Fatso (*see* cats in Cuba)
Feather Kcat (*see* cats in Toronto)
Feather Kitty (*see* cats in Cuba)
Feather Puss (*see* cats in Paris)
Ferro, Gladys Rodriguez, 95, 162, 163
Fig tree (Key West), 33, 43
Finca cats (*see* cats in Cuba)
Finca Vigia (Lookout Farm), **ii**, **v**, **viii**, **ix**, **x**, **43**, 44, 45, **45**, 46, **47**, 48, **48**, 49, 50, **53**, 55, 60, 62, 65, 70, 71, 72, **72**, 73, **75**, 77, 81, 82, 83, **83**, **86**, 88, **89**, 93, 95, 98, 101, 102, **102**, **103**, **104**, **105**, **106**, 107, **107**, **108**, 109, 111, **112**, 113, 115, **118**, **119**, 120, **123**, 129, **129**, **130**, 131, 133, 136, 137, 140, 144, **145**, 147, **147**, 153, 159, 160, 161, 162, **162**, 163, 165, 166, 167, 168, 169, 170, 171
Fitzgerald, F. Scott, 24
Flandre, 115
Florence, Italy, 10
Floridita Bar and Restaurant, Cuba, 59
For Whom the Bell Tolls, 42, 45, 73, 75, 186
Franco, Francisco, 42
Friendless (*see* cats in Cuba)
Friendless' Brother (*see* cats in Cuba)
Fuentes, Gregorio, 128, 162, 163
Furhouse (*see* cats in Cuba)

G

Garden of Eden, The, 3, 67, 99, 113, 118, 119, 139, 148, 172, 183

Gardner, Carol Hemingway (*see* Hemingway, Carol (sister)

Gellhorn, Martha (*see* Hemingway, Martha Gellhorn)

Gigi (*see* Hemingway, Gregory Hancock)

Goats (*see* cats in Cuba)

Good Will (*see* cats in Cuba)

Gordon, Ruth, 29

Green Hills of Africa, 115

Guanabacoa, Cuba, 50

Guardia Rural, 138

H

Hall, Caroline Hancock (grandmother), 2

Hall, Ernest Abba (grandfather), 2, **2**, 173

Havana, Cuba, 41, 44, 57, 58, 81, 125, 136, 144, **144**, 160

Hemingway, Alfred Tyler (uncle), 9

Hemingway, Anson T. (grandfather), 67

Hemingway, Carol (daughter-in-law), 36

Hemingway, Carol (sister), 5, 6, 13, **13**, 29

Hemingway, Clarence "Ed" Edmonds (father), **xiv**, 1, 2, 3, **3**, 6, 13, **13**, 28, 62, 169

Hemingway, Doris (daughter-in-law), 79

Hemingway, Ernest Miller, **12**, **13**, **14**, **16**, **18**, **22**, **23**, **25**, **46**, **48**, **53**, **54**, **61**, **68**, **74**, **81**, **91**, **111**, **116**, **117**, **143**, **158**

African safari (1933–34), 67, 115, 120

African safari (1953–54), 115, 116, 136

ambulance driver in Italy, 9, 10

animal doctoring, 2, 140

animals and valuable aid, 36, 48, 107, 169, 180

airplane crashes, 117, 121, 122, **122**, 123

automobiles, 26, 27, 99, 101

boxing, 45

bravery, 10

Bronze Star (*see* Hemingway, Ernest, World War II)

bullfights, 29, 31, 144, 147, 148, 149

Catholic burial, 155

childhood, **xiv**, 1, **1**, 2, **2**, 3, **3**, **4**, 5–7, **7**, **66**

Cuban revolution, 89, 144, 159, 160, 161

death of Black Dog, **134**, 135, **135**, 136

death of Boise, 127–131

death of friends and family, 107, 137

dining with his cats, **vi**, **viii**, 55, **55**, 83, 149, **150**, **151**, **163**, 165, 166

divorces, 23, 24, 43, 76, 79

drinking, 45, 72, 128

education, 9

F.B.I., 153

fishing, 5, 6, 10, **27**, 70, 111, 122

early years, 10

Cuba, 70, 111

Key West, **26**, 27, **27**, **32**

Marlin fishing in Peru, 128-129

German submarines, 69–73, **69**, **70**

health of,

accidents, 79, 99, 155

back injuries, 122, 128

blood pressure, 99, 151

depression, 139, 148, 151, 173

diabetes, type II, 151

failing health, 153

head injuries, 99, 121, 123

kidney problems, 122, 123, 127, 151

liver disease, 123, 127, 151

mental illness, 147, 148, 151, 160

nervous breakdown, 128, 148, 160

shock treatments, 151, 153

horses, fondness of, 2

journalism, 9, 15, 19

Kansas City Star, 9

loss of Finca Vigia, 153

loss of manuscripts, 20

naturalist, 2, 121

Nobel Prize, 125, **125**, 137
on hunting, 67
on war, 70
political beliefs, 153
Pulitzer Prize, 24, 111, 113
rescuing unwanted animals, 2
sex life, 91
sports, love of,
  boxing, 45
  skiing, 92, 100
  tennis, 55
suicide of, 155, 156
teenage years, 5–7
wanting a daughter, 29, 39, 40, 72, 91
war correspondent,
  Spanish Civil War, 42, 69
  World War II, 74, 77
weight, 101
wild animals, understanding of, 140
without his cats, 151, 153
World War I, 9, 10, **11**
  medals, 10
  war wounds, **8**, 10, 45
World War II, 73, 74, 75
  injuries, 79
  medals, 95
writing,
  adult, 15, 16, 19, 21, 25, 28, 74,
    91, 99,
  after injuries, 99, 127, 128
  after shock treatments, 151
  early years, 9
  with the company of animals, **ii**, **iii**, **v**,
    ix, **x**, 21, 47, 49, 51, **56**, **64**, 76,
    85, 86, **90**, **94**, 97, **97**, **98**, **100**,
    101, 109, **110**, **112**, **114**, **123**,
    126, 128, **137**, **138**, **141**, **145**,
    148, 152, **154**, 165, 166, 167,
    169, **174**
Hemingway, Grace Hall (mother), **xiv**, 1,
  2, 3, **3**, **4**, 5, 6, 7, **7**, 13, **13**, 29, 66,
  107
Hemingway, Gregory Hancock (son), **v**,
  29, 33, 34, **34**, 35, **35**, 36, **37**, 43, 48,
  48, 49, 50, 51, **51**, **52**, 62, **62**, 63,

66, 107
Hemingway, Hadley Richardson (first
  wife), **12**, 13, **14**, 15, 16, 17, 19, 20,
  20, 21, **21**, 23, 24, **25**, 27, 28, 42, 60,
  62, 72, 100, 139, 156, 167, 173
Hemingway, Hilary Hancock (niece), **x**,
  151
Hemingway, John Hadley Nicanor
  "Bumby" (son), **18**, 19, 20, 21, **21**,
  24, **25**, 27, 28, 29, 47, **62**, 72, 100,
  115, 167, 173
Hemingway, Leicester (brother), 5, 13, **13**,
  29, 73, 79, 133, 135, 183
  affair with Mary Welsh, 73
Hemingway, Madelaine "Sunny" (sister),
  xiv, 1, 3, **3**, 5, 6, 13, **13**, 28, 29, 66,
  83, 97, 184
Hemingway, Marcelline (sister), **xiv**, 1, 2,
  2, 3, **3**, **4**, 5, 13, **13**, 29, 43, 66, 185
Hemingway, Martha Gellhorn (third wife),
  39, **39**, 40, **40**, 41, 42, 43, **43**, 44, 45,
  47, 49, 51, 55, 57, 63, 65, 70, 71, 72,
  73, 75, 76, 77, 79, 81, 82, 83, 113,
  133, 156, 165, 169, 170, 182
Hemingway, Mary Welsh (fourth wife), **ix**,
  73, 74, 76, **78**, **80**, 81, **81**, 82, **82**, 83,
  83, 86, 87, 89, 91, **91**, 92, 97, 99, **99**,
  100, 101, 102, 107, 109, 111, 112,
  113, 114, **114**, 115, **116**, 117, **117**,
  119, 120, 121, 122, 123, 125,128,
  129, 130, 131, 133, 135, 136, 139,
  140, 141, 143, 144, 147, 149, 151,
  152, 153, 155, 156, 159, 160, 161,
  162, 163, 165, 166, 167, 168, 169,
  170, 171, 172, 173
Hemingway, Patricia Shedd (sister-in-law),
  79, 183
Hemingway, Patrick (son), **v**, 28, 30, 33,
  34, **35**, 36, **37**, 43, **48**, 48, 49, **50**,
  52, **62**, 63, 65, 70, 71, 92, 100, 120,
  122, 140, 153, 155, 156, 165, 168,
  171, 178
Hemingway, Pauline Pfeiffer (second wife),
  22, **23**, 23–25, **26**, 27, 28, 29, 33, 36,
  39–40, 42, 43, 61–62, 107, 115, 120

Hemingway, Sean (grandson), 28, 30, 33, 34, 35, 36, 37, 43, 48, 49, 50, 52, 62, 63, 65, 70, 71, 92, 100, 120, 122, 140, 153, 155, 156, 168, 171, 178, 187

Hemingway, Ursula (sister), **xiv**, 2, **2**, 3, **3**, **4**, 13, **13**, 29, 66, **66**

Hemingway, Valerie (daughter-in-law), 77, 136, 147, 148, **148**, 149, 153, 159, 169, 178, 183

Herald, Matthew, 23

Herrera, Dr. Jose Luis, 159, 161

Herrera, Roberto, 159

Hindmarsh, Harry, 19

Horne, Bill, 13

horses, 2

Horton Bay, Michigan, 13

Hotchner, Aaron Edward "A.E.," 66, 101, 134, 139, 140, 142

Hudson, Thomas, 45, 48, 50, 55, 59, 60, 70, 81, 82, 96, 97, 127, 139, 156

Humane Society, Toronto, 19

I

Ile de France, 40, 74

In Our Time, 17, 186

Isabella la Católica (*see* cats in Cuba)

Isabella, Queen of Spain, 133

Islands in the Stream, 3, 7, 34, 39, 45, 47, 49, 50, 51, 55, 57, 60, 65, 69, 70, 79, 81, 91, 96, 97, 107, 109, 113, 125, 127, 128, 131, 139, 155, 156, 165, 167, 168, 169, 170, 171, 172, 173, 187

Ivancich, Adriana, 111, **111**, 113, 114, 120, 125, 137, 139, 144

Ivancich, Dora, 111

Ivancich, Gianfranco, 111, 113, 115, 131, 137, 144, 156

Izzy (*see* cats in Cuba)

Izzy the Cat (*see* cats in Cuba)

J

Joan of Arc, 123

K

Kansas City, Missouri, 28, 29

Kansas City Star, 9

Kennedy, President John F., 159

Kenya, 116, 136, 173

Kert, Bernice, 25, 28, 41

Ketchum, Idaho, 92, 100, 101, 107, 139, 140, **141**, 142, **142**, 143, 147, **148**, 149, 151, 153, 155, **155**, 159, 162, 165, 169, 170, 172, 174

Key West, Florida, **x**, 26, 27, 28, 29, **30**, 31, **31**, 33, **33**, 34, 35, **35**, 36, **36**, 37, 38, 40, 41, **43**, 154, 162

Key West Lighthouse, 29

Kibo (*see* dogs in Africa)

Kilimanjaro, 117

Kipling, Rudyard, 5

Kitanga Farm, Africa, 117

L

Lake Tanganyika, Tanzania, 120

Lake Victoria Hotel, Entebbe, 122

Landon, Colonel C.T. "Buck," 74

Langosta (fisherman), 62

Lansky, Meyer, 144

Lassie (*see* dogs in Hollywood)

La Terraza Restaurant and Bar, Cojimar, 49

Lausanne, Switzerland, 20

Left Bank, Paris, 15

L'Eglise de St. Honore d'Eylau, 24

Le Grau-du-Roi, France, 24

Lem (*see* dogs in Cuba)

L'Hôtel Jacob et d'Angleterre, 15

Life magazine, 147

Liana, 71

Littless Kitty (*see* cats in Cuba)

Liverpool, England, 73

London, England, 71, 73, 74

Look magazine, 115

Lookout Farm (*see* Finca Vigia)

Luxembourg Gardens, Paris, 20

M

MacDonald Cabins, 92, 100

Machakos (*see* dogs in Cuba)

Machakos, Kenya, 117
MacLeish, Archibald "Archie," 136
MacMullen, Forrest "Duke," **141**, 143
Madrid, Spain, 42, 115, 148
Malaga, Spain, 144
Malecon, Havana, 144
Manx (*see* cats in Oak Park)
Marie (femme de ménage in Paris), 21
Mario (houseboy in *Islands in the Stream*), 60, 61
Marita (love interest in *The Garden of Eden*), 148
Marseilles, France, 115
Marsh, Roy, 121
Masindi, Uganda, 121
Mason, Grant, 178
Mason, Jane Kendall, 36, 40, **40**, 41, 42
Mayo Clinic, 151, 153, 156
Mellow, James, 10, 184
Men at War, 69
Men without Women, 27
Menocal, Mayito, 115, 120
Mery, Dr. Ferdinand, 1, 184
Meyers, Art, 13
Miami, Florida, 33
Miami Beach, Florida, 144
Miami Herald, The, 33
Milan, Italy, 10
Miller, Madelaine "Sunny" Hemingway (*see* Hemingway, Madelaine "Sunny")
Miss Kitty (*see* cats in Idaho and out West)
Mombassa, Kenya, 115
Monks, Noel, 73
Montmartre, Paris, 17
Mooky (*see* cats in Idaho and out West)
Moorehead, Caroline, 156
Moose (*see* Hemingway, Patrick)
Morris, Desmond, 47, 184
Moveable Feast, A, 3, 15, 19, 21, 23, 24, 100, 139, 140, 167, 173, 187
Mowrer, Hadley Richardson (*see* Hemingway, Hadley Richardson)
Mowrer, Paul Scott, 24, 25, 156
and Pulitzer Prize, 24

Mr. Willy (*see* cats in Cuba)
Mundo (caretaker of cows in Cuba), 144
Murchison Falls, Africa, 121
Murphy, Baoth, 156
Murphy, Gerald, 42, 43, 157
Murphy, Patrick, 156
Murphy, Sara Sherman Wiborg, 42, 43, 79, 156, **156**, 157
Murray, Utah, 92, 169
Museo Ernest Hemingway, Cuba, 108

N
Nagel, Dr. James, 11
Nairobi, Kenya, 117
Natural History of the World, A, 9
Negrita (*see* dogs in Cuba)
New York City, 10, 28, 45, 66, 73, 89, 107, 123, 144, 147, 149
New York Post, 89
New York Times, The, 123
Normandy, France, 74
North American Newspaper Alliance, 42
North, John Ringling, 66
Now I Lay Me, 5
Nuisance Value (*see* cats in Cuba)

O
Oak Park, Illinois, 1, **1**, 5, **5**, 9, 28, 67
Oak Park and River Forest Township High School, 9
Oak Park Library, 5
Oberlin College, 9
Office of Strategic Services, 74
Old Man and the Sea, The, 111, 113, 114, 127, 137, 164
Ondaatje, Christopher, 42, 74, 184
operation Friendless, 69
Owlry (great horned owl in Idaho), 140, **140**, **141**, 174, **174**

P
Pamplona, Spain, 31, 115
Paris, France, 14, 15, 16, 17, 18, 19, 20, 21, **21**, 24, 27, 47, 56, 57, 60, 74, 89, 139, 156

Paris, SS, 42

peacocks in Key West, 33

Pelusa (*see* cats in Cuba)

Pentecost, Jack, 13

Percival, Philip, 115, 119, 120, 136, 178

Perkins, Maxwell "Max," 24, 29, 45, 99, 107, 139

Pfeiffer, Augustus "Gus," 26, 27, 29

Pfeiffer, Pauline (*see* Hemingway, Pauline Pfeiffer)

Pfeiffer, Virginia "Jinny," 23, 24

Piggott, Arkansas, 23

Pilar (*see* Hemingway, Pauline Pfeiffer)

Pilar (Hemingway's boat), 68, 69, 70, 71, 81, 111, 162

Pollard, Michael, 65

Pony (*see* cats in Cuba)

Pound, Ezra, 19

Powell, Dawn, 73

Prieto, Abel (Cuban Minister of Culture), 161

Princessa (*see* cats in Cuba)

R

Rapallo, Italy, 16

Red Cross, 9, 10

Red Cross Nursing Service, 10

Reynolds, Michael, 21, 28, 40, 43, 91, 120, 121, 185

Rhone River, France, 24

Rice, Alfred, 159

Richardson, Hadley (*see* Hemingway, Hadley Richardson)

Ringling Brothers Circus, 66

Ritz, Paris, 74

Riva, Maria, 111

Rivero, Edwardo, 87

Rockefeller, Nelson, 50, 72, 168

Rollyson, Carl, 41, 185

Rome, Dr. Howard, 151, 153

Roosevelt, Teddy, 67, 115

Rotonde café, Paris, 15

Royal Air Force, 74

Rush Medical College, 9

Russell, Joe "Josie," 41

Russo-Japanese War, 66

S

Salvation Army, 136

San Francisco de Paula, Cuba, 45, 87

San Sebastian, Spain, 23

Sanford, Marcelline Hemingway (*see* Hemingway, Marcelline)

Saviers, Dr. George, 151

Schnauz (*see* dogs in Austria)

Schruns, Austria, 100

Scribner, Charles, 24, 107, 139

Selby Hotel, Toronto, 19

Shakespeare (*see* cats in Cuba)

Shakespeare and Co. Bookstore, 20

Shaw, Irwin, 79

Shedd, Patricia, (*see* Hemingway, Patricia Shedd)

Shimoni, Kenya, 122

Shopsky (*see* cats in Cuba)

Short Happy Life of Francis Macomber, The, 65

Siberia, Russia, 86

Silver Dawn Cattery, 47, 72, 169

Sir Winston Churchill (*see* cats in Cuba)

Sister Kitty (*see* cats in Idaho and out West)

Sloppy Joe's Bar, Key West, 33, 39, 41, **41**

Smelly (*see* cats in Cuba)

Smith, Bill, 13

Smith, Katy (*see* Dos Passos, Katy Smith)

snakes, 119, 120

Snowball (*see* cats in Key West)

Snow Leopard (*see* cats in Cuba)

Sokoloff, Alice Hunt, 20, 24, 185

Spain, 144, 147, 149

Spendthrift (*see* cats in Cuba)

Spendy (*see* cats in Cuba)

Stein, Gertrude, 19, 20, 24, 107

Steinbeck, John, 69

Stephen Spender (*see* cats in Cuba)

Stevenson, Robert Louis, 5

Stobbs (*see* cats in Cuba)

St. Louis, Missouri, 13

St. Mary's Hospital, Rochester, Minnesota, 151

Stoopy (*see* cats in Cuba)
Stoopy Wolfer (*see* cats in Cuba)
Stranger (*see* cats in Cuba)
Sun Also Rises, The, 24
Sun Valley, Idaho, 91, 92, 99, 139, 157

T
Tabula (Oak Park High School magazine), 9
Taskforce (*see* cats in Cuba)
Tassel (*see* dogs in Oak Park)
Taube Hotel, Schruns, Austria, 100, 173
Tester (*see* cats in Cuba)
Theisen, Earl, 115, 120
Thomas, Hugh, 159, 186
Thompson, Charles, 67, 120
Three Mountain Press, 16, 186
Three Stories and Ten Poems, 16, 186
Thruster (*see* cats in Cuba)
Thrusty (*see* cats in Cuba)
Time magazine, 17, 73
Toronto, Canada, 19
Toronto Daily Star, 13, 15
Toklas, Alice B., 24
To Have and Have Not, 39
Torrents of Spring, The, 24, 27
Tracey, Spencer, 127
Trapeze, The, 9
Trevor and Morris Ford Agency, 27
True at First Light, 3, 117, 119, 120, 121, 127, 139, 155, 187
Twain, Mark, 5
Twysden, Lady Duff, 24, 41

U
Uncle Willy (*see* cats in Cuba)
Uncle Wolfer (*see* cats in Cuba)
Uncle Wolfie (*see* cats in Cuba)
Union Pacific, 92
United States embargo of Cuba, 57, 159
Upper Michigan, 5, 6, 13, 24

V
Vaill, Amanda, 42, 186
Venice, Italy, 113, 120, 156

Verlaine, Paul, 15
Viking, Madonna, (*see* Murphy, Sara Sherman Wiborg)
Villiard, Henry S., 9, 11, 186
Villarreal, Rene, 83, 109, 115, 144, **145**, 159, 162
Vogue magazine, 23
von Kurowsky, Agnes Hannah, 9, **9**, 10, 11, 24, 28, 186

W
Walloon Lake, Upper Michigan, **4**, 5, 10, 13, **13**, 66
Washington, D.C., 10, 153
Wax Puppy (*see* dogs in Paris)
Welsh, Mary (*see* Hemingway, Mary Welsh)
White Tower Restaurant, London, 79
White, William, 100, 187
Will (*see* cats in Cuba)
Willie (*see* cats in Cuba)
Willy (*see* cats in Cuba)
Wilson, Earl, 89
Windermere cottage, Upper Michigan, 5, 7, 10, 13
Wolfer (*see* cats in Cuba)

Z
Zaphiro, Dennis, 117, 120, 172

Here are some other books from Pineapple Press on related topics. For a complete catalog, write to Pineapple Press, P.O. Box 3889, Sarasota, Florida 34230-3889, or call (800) 746-3275. Or visit our website at www.pineapplepress.com.

Hemingway's Key West, Second Edition, by Stuart McIver. This vivid portrait reveals both Hemingway, the writer, and Hemingway, the macho, hard-drinking sportsman. Includes a two-hour walking tour of his favorite Key West haunts. (pb)

My Brother, Ernest Hemingway by Leicester Hemingway. First published in 1962, this updated edition includes a selection of letters from Ernest to his family never before published. If you want to know who Ernest Hemingway really was, you need to read what his brother had to say about him. (hb)

The Horses of Proud Spirit by Melanie Sue Bowles. The wonderful story of one of the most successful and longest running horse sanctuaries in the United States. At Proud Spirit, horses that arrive after being neglected or abused finally know safety, affection, and the companionship of other horses. This moving memoir of lessons learned in compassion, strength, and loss is an homage to the spirit of these alluring creatures. (hb)

Hoof Prints: More Stories from Proud Spirit by Melanie Sue Bowles. Learn more about the compelling recoveries of abused and abandoned horses when they come to Proud Spirit Sanctuary. (hb)

The Dogs of Proud Spirit by Melanie Sue Bowles. Unforgettable true stories of the homeless and stray dogs who have found a loving home at Proud Spirit Horse Sanctuary. (hb)

The Houses of Key West by Alex Caemmerer. This book offers a selection of what are probably the most historically interesting, esthetically appealing, and photogenic of the nineteenth-century houses in the Key West historic district. Some are examples of well-known architectural styles, whereas others were completely individually conceived. (pb)

The Streets of Key West by J. Wills Burke. Simonton, Duval, Eaton, Whitehead, Southard, Truman—if you discover how these Key West streets, and all the others, came by their names, you will know much of the history of this little island at the nethermost end of the continental United States. You will learn of the rise and fall and rise again of the fortunes of this island town, which has played such a rich role in the history of the country as a whole. (hb)

Over Key West and the Florida Keys by Charles Feil. Full-color aerial shots of shimmering ocean, uninhabited mangrove islands, bridges and causeways, vintage neighborhoods, and million-dollar homes. An appealing blend of descriptive text and dreamy images that capture the beauty and uniqueness of the Florida Keys. A beautiful coffee-table book. (hb)